| Dedication

To Jim and Cathy. Anything good I do in this life is by God's grace and because you are my parents

CONTENTS

Introduction

1   Goldfish   7

2   Messed Up   21

3   Rich   42

4   Idle Worship   61

5   Excuses   76

6   Money   97

7   Sacrifice   110

8   Go And Do Likewise   129

9   Surrendering the American Dream   139

10 Don't Be a Goat   152

Conclusion

| Introduction

I take it as a personal challenge each time we buy groceries to carry all of them into our house in as few loads as possible. Nothing brings my macho ego more satisfaction then plopping nineteen plastic bags on the kitchen counter at once. Never mind that all the circulation has been cut off to my fingertips or that I speed-waddled into the house with the grace of an overburdened pack mule. I have accomplished something mere mortals can only dream of.

   To carry seventeen plastic bags, two sacks of potatoes, three cases of soda, and a 48-roll pack of toilet paper into my house in one trip and and barely break a sweat is the pinnacle of manliness.

Please, hold your applause.

There are risks involved, of course. If I drop something, there's no way I can stop to pick it up. If I get an itch on my nose, there's no way I can free up a finger to scratch it. Occasionally, the rest of the family forgets that I'm busy carrying in the groceries like a boss, and they forget to hold the door. This means I'll be kicking at the glass impatiently while losing the feeling in my forearms until someone comes to my aid.

My hands are so full, my grip so tight, there is no way I can do a single other thing.

Sometimes our faith is like that.

Sometimes we cling to some things so tightly it is impossible for us to take hold of anything else. Like me and my grocery-carrying obsession, we're preoccupied and overburdened and we don't have the luxury of latching on to one more thing. Our grip is being tested as it is.

But what if by clutching one thing we're missing out on something more important?

Imagine me with both hands stuffed with groceries, my knuckles white with tension. Now imagine my son coming out to hold the door for me but tripping on his way out and falling head first into the glass. He starts screaming and bleeding and wailing and rolling around. It's bad.

Real bad.

Now imagine me clutching my groceries, staring down at my son, and saying, "Sorry, bud. Not much I can do. I know it's important, but I got my hands full here."

That sounds insane, right? Inexcusable even. A call to protective services may be in order. An itchy nose is one thing. A crisis like a bleeding kid, you don't wait. You drop everything and you attend to the more urgent need.

Is it possible that we're living out our faith like that? We've got a tight grip on something and when a more pressing issue arises we can't turn loose long enough to engage? We're just holding on too tightly.

"Sorry, bud. Not much I can do. Got my hands full here."

1 Timothy 6:17-19 says,

> "As for the rich in this present age, charge them not to be haughty, nor to set their hopes on the uncertainty of riches, but on

God, who richly provides us with everything to enjoy. They are to do good, to be rich in good works, to be generous and ready to share, thus storing up treasure for themselves as a good foundation for the future, so that they may take hold of that which is truly life."

Let me be very clear with you from the start.

In the pages that follow, I'm going to attempt to convince you to loosen your grip on your life of luxury and comfort in order to dig a little deeper and take hold of what Paul says is "the life that is truly life."

I'm not going to be a jerk about it. I'm learning as I go and I'm not exactly an expert on unselfishness. I am not going to beat around the bush, either. I think the Scriptures are pretty clear on the mandate to be as generous as we possibly can, and I think we're all called to respond.

I am anticipating some objections, and I hope to treat all those with the same respect I would if we were sitting across from one another as friends sipping on some coffee. I've heard a lot of them over the years, and I just can't help but think that they miss the point. The bottom line for me is simple: Jesus Himself had and commands us to likewise have a steadfast, fervent, passionate concern for the poor.

For too long, a lot of us have held on to faulty values too tightly and used them as an excuse to not dig a little deeper and take hold of something much more valuable. Instead of strengthening our grip on what it is we're clutching, perhaps a better response would be to let loose.

It was the early church father Augustine who said, "God is always trying to give good things to us, but our hands are too full to receive them."

This is a book for people whose hands are too full. Maybe it's with stuff or comfort or ambition or plans, but our knuckles are white from the burden. This is a book for people who are willing to take a long look in the mirror and ask some tough questions. This is a book for people who look at how messed up the world is and get an ache in their gut as a result. This is a book for people who are convinced that the people of God should be the most generous people on earth. This is a book for people who are feeling stale in their faith but can't quite figure out why. This is a book for people who aren't afraid to take risks that some might consider foolish. This is a book for people who don't think serving the poor is extra credit, but a foundational response to the Gospel. To do nothing is not a viable option.

This is a book for all of us, because none of us as Christ followers are exempt. All of us are called to let loose, dig deep, and take hold.

1 | Goldfish

"Whoever closes his ear to the cry of the poor will himself call out and not be answered." Proverbs 21:13

On January 12, 2010, at 4:53 p.m. a 7.0 magnitude earthquake rocked the brittle foundation of the nation of Haiti. It demolished buildings and toppled the already fragile hope of the inhabitants of the poorest country in the western hemisphere.

Thirty-three aftershocks followed, each of which registered at least a 4.2 on the Richter scale. Three million people were instantly in need of emergency aid. Over 225,000 are estimated to have died. An additional 300,000-plus were injured.

My wife and I were discussing the tragedy at home one night when my five-year-old daughter overheard us talking. She started asking questions about Haiti and we tried to explain how it was a poor country where people didn't have everything they needed. As my little girl heard stories about what they were dealing with in that country, she was moved to action. She also had a lot of questions.

Finally, she just came out and stated the obvious. It didn't make any sense to her that people in Haiti would have so *little* when we had so *much*. "Much" is a relative term, I know. At the time my family lived in about a 1,100 square foot house. I was a student pastor. My wife was a nurse. We had what we needed, but not much else. To some, we didn't have "much." To the residents of Haiti, we may as well have been Bill and Melinda Gates.

We'd been discussing what we could give. Our church had a relationship with a missionary couple there, and we were taking up a special offering for the recovery work. I don't know if it confused her why we had to take up an offering or what, but she was not okay with the fact that the people in Haiti were suffering. As we went into the kitchen to retrieve a snack one night she articulated one of the questions she was having trouble answering most.

"Why doesn't God just give the people what they need?" It was a valid question, one most people have asked at one point or another. She wasn't asking out of a position of doubt. She knew God was powerful. She knew He had blessed us with more than we needed. What she didn't understand was why He hadn't done the same for everyone. Even now, several years later, her innocent question resonates with me. It probably does with you, too. Why *does* God allow that kind of inequity?

My daughter and I sat down at our dining room table to eat a snack, and I opened up a bag of those goldfish crackers, dropping an enormous handful in front of her eager little fingers. I mean I had never been so generous as I was that evening. Then I gave myself a single cracker. She stared at my minuscule snack but paid me little attention. She began to eat and after one bite I quickly ran out.

I sat there for a while and then I started asking

some questions of my own.

"Why do you think God let me have one cracker when you have so many?" I asked.

She just looked at me. You would love my daughter if you knew her. Beautiful eyes like her mom. She really is a treat to be around. On this night, her charm was irrelevant to me. I had an important lesson to teach.

"Do you think it's unfair that you have so many crackers and I don't have any?"

I could see on her face that she was making a loose connection. Still, she munched away. I sat in silence for a while.

"I wish I had more to eat," I mumbled under my breath to no one in particular.

"Just get more out of the bag," she suggested, pointing at the bag on the table. Smart kid. She must've been hungry or something. When I shook the empty bag in front of her face she knew her solution would not work, however.

I was quiet a little longer so my daughter could think. Then I started to lay it on thick.

"I'm just so hungry. If there were only some more crackers *somewhere* I could have more. God is so unjust to only give me one cracker. How could

God do this to me?"

I knew a five year old probably didn't know what "unjust" meant, but she was learning as the seconds ticked by. I kept my foot on the gas.

"If God really loved me, I would have more crackers. I don't have what I need. I need more to eat. It's God's fault! It's God's fault I don't have any more to eat!"

To this day I don't know if my daughter was just tired of hearing me whine or if she was starting to get the point, but I did see a little flicker in her eye. She stared at her mound of goldfish. She had started with so many that she had barely put a dent in the pile at this stage.

Then she looked at me. I thought I saw a trace of sympathetic recognition in her flat smile.

"What?" I asked, feigning ignorance. I wasn't going to make her do anything.

Slowly, she reached down and grabbed a single goldfish. She pressed it between her index finger and the table and slowly scooted it in front of me. She repeated the gesture several times. Then, as she realized how much I appreciated her generosity, she scooped up a small handful of goldfish crackers in her chubby palms and dumped them in front of me. I don't even like those things that much, but I ate every one of them that night.

My daughter learned an important lesson that night, and I did too. Perhaps for the first time, I realized I was holding a fistful of crackers--and there was a whole mess of people around the world who were hungry for a snack. Most of my life I had just expected them to reach in and get more out of the bag while I chomped away at my abundance.

The problem was not God's injustice. The problem was my clenched fist.

I didn't grow up with much.

My dad labored tirelessly on a farm he did not own; my mother drove a school bus. We never missed a meal, but I feel like we may have come close a few times. I was too busy loving my life to notice. The "luxuries" we enjoyed now seem so basic. My basketball goal was the round wooden end to a large commercial wire spool that barely measured three feet across. My dad detached it from the spool and mounted it to a hefty tree branch. Our swimming pool was a corrugated steel tank normally reserved for watering livestock. It got a little scuzzy now and then, but we never minded much.

The majority of my childhood was spent in a small town isolated on a plateau in the south-central section of Missouri, thirty minutes from everywhere else. Most families stayed there forever, but some came and went. Natives thought of the "imports" as an intrusion. To me it was a chance to make a new friend.

In about fourth grade Jason started going to my elementary school. His family moved to town or at least to our side of town, I don't remember which. Jason was shorter than most of the boys and even some of the girls, and a skinny strand of hair ran down the back of his neck.

Jason had a rattail, and I instantly wanted one.

We became pretty good friends because he was fast and I wanted to be. In fourth grade the kids who are decent at sports usually form a peer group, and this was the cluster I ran with. Jason joined us for recess basketball games and was one of the first kids picked for kickball and softball and pretty much any other sport when we played them in gym class.

He had a hot temper. According to the tales he spun of his previous macho victories, Jason was not to be crossed. He talked tough, with fouler language than any fourth grader should possess. I experimented with some of the words to see if I would sound as tough as he did, but it all came across sort of phony.

It didn't keep me from trying.

Jason got into a brawl or two, and the legend of his strength grew. I wondered if that was why he was in our school now. Perhaps he had been suspended from the others due to violent explosions. The longer he was with us the more I came to believe that he could whip a boy twice his size without much trouble. He could probably defeat a foe with one crack of his ample rattail. I secretly vowed never to make him angry.

Our school didn't serve up much at lunchtime that I looked forward to. I was on the free meal plan, so I ate what I was given and didn't complain. Some of the combinations served tested my resolve, though.

There was the All-Brown Meal. It included a grilled cheese sandwich toasted to a golden brown with a side of brown tater tots and gooey brown applesauce. I always got chocolate milk, so it was brown too. If one of the lunch ladies scooted me a brown tray it was hard to tell where the entree ended and a side dish began. Didn't really matter, though. It tasted decent enough despite its lack of color. You fry anything long enough it becomes edible. I routinely cleared my plate.

Then there was Goulash Day. Our "Goulash" was sort of like spaghetti but more mysterious, and this was not a day I looked forward to. I picked through it as best I could, consuming the less ambiguous ingredients. On these days all-class trade negotiations would take place--my goulash for your lettuce salad, my chocolate milk for a treat you brought from home, etc. If I were shrewd and persistent, I would get up from the lunch table moderately satisfied--even on Goulash Day.

Then there was Crispito Day.

Crispito Day was like lunchroom Christmas. Crispitos were everyone's favorite. Crispitos made me forget that there *was* such a thing as Goulash Day. On Crispito Day all was right with the world.

Basically a burrito but fried thin and crispy, Crispitos were in high demand and low supply. I still don't know why we only got one each. I could easily consume three. Trades kicked off as soon as we entered the lunchroom. I'm not even kidding. The cafeteria resembled the floor of the New York Stock Exchange as soon as word made it back from the front of the line what was being served.

On Crispito Day, I was uncharacteristically aggressive. I had a mental list of the girls who did not like Crispitos (how could you not like *Crispitos!*) and from whom I could receive one for free. I was willing to deal off all side dishes in order to build up my plate with gently fried "beef" and beans wrapped in a supernaturally delicious tortilla. I would consider two for one trades, barter non-food items, and offer a variety of personal services. Don't judge me. You have probably never enjoyed a Crispito. If you had, you'd be nodding your head in agreement.

On a good day, I would land four or five Crispitos. On a tough day, if I was toward the back of the line or distracted by a fifth grade girl who may have smiled at me earlier in the day, I would have to settle for two or three total. Those were bad days. Seriously, you guys. Crispitos were amazing.

I'll never forget the day that Jason almost whipped me good. It was Crispito Day, and I had enjoyed a very effective hunt. Everything had gone my way. I was toward the front of the line and by the time I sat down, I had already secured a total of four Crispitos *for free*. I then dealt my sides with efficiency and gained three more. By the time my whole class was seated, I was the excited owner of *seven* Crispitos and ready to dig in. It was a two-fisted Crispito kind of day. Life was good.

Then Jason walked by.

"Where'd you get all those?" he asked.

I recalled my Crispito conquest like a proud American General who'd just taken an entire battlefield.

"Let me have one," Jason suggested, without a trace of anger. Just a friend assuming his buddy would be willing to share. I mean, I did have a lot of them.

Still consumed with adrenaline from my cheesy, crispy conquest, I politely refused. This is America. You get what you work for. What am I, a charity?

Jason's face began to redden and I realized my

error. Memories of details he'd shared with me of lesser warriors he had vanquished sprung to my mind. But it was too late to back track. I had to stand my ground, or risk losing *all* my loot during his overreaction.

"It's only *fair*," he insisted, playing the trump card for any fourth grade argument. "You have seven and I only have one. Just give me one more."

I was blinded by my appetite and self-centeredness. I refused a second time, adding with boldness, "Get your *own* Crispitos."

I am certain this is not the case, but in my memory I build up the drama considerably. It goes something like this: The entire cafeteria is hushed while various blonde-headed girls whisper to one another about valor and grit. The boys begin to take bets on who will blink first, and I rise to my feet to meet Jason's challenge, a Crispito in each hand, like a couple of greasy nun chucks. It was high noon and we were a couple of gunslingers in the Wild West.

What *really* happened was Jason didn't like my tone one bit. He stared me down and said with conviction; "Don't cop an attitude with *me*."

It was his last warning.

"I'll cop an attitude with anyone I want," I said,

unflinching. Was it my hunger or my naivety fueling this bravery? I couldn't decide.

For reasons unknown to me this day, Jason simply walked away. He sat and ate his Crispito in defeat while I feasted on seven of 'em with a smug look of satisfaction on my face. I had stood up to the rat-tailed bully and lived to tell about it. Better still, I had retained possession of all seven Crispitos.

Even today as I tell you that story I don't like that version of myself. In fact, I don't think I enjoyed that moment any longer than it took me to eat my lunch. After that, I just felt like a bully, and I still do.

I tell you about the earthquake and the crackers and the Crispitos and my confrontation with Jason for a singular reason. I am convicted of the following truth and that the following truth should alter our attitudes and the way we live out our lives. It was true with the goldfish, it was true in the lunchroom, and it's still true in Haiti and a thousand other places around the world today.

There's something else that's true, though, that I can't go on without saying--there is plenty to go around and only selfish jerks refuse to share.

2 | Messed Up

"In this world you will have trouble. But take heart; I have overcome the world." Jesus, John 16:33

Lest you think "selfish jerks" is too strong a word choice, let me be the first to raise my hand and volunteer to wear that label. Unfortunately, I've not changed much since the Crispito incident. I still keep a pretty tight grip on certain things.

I get pretty grumpy when my kids raid the pantry and tear into chips I intended to eat. I still use the word "mine" to describe lots of things I keep in my house. And I'm definitely stingy with my time. I covet the peace and quiet that comes with a couple of uninterrupted hours, and I don't easily surrender it to anyone for any reason.

Some people keep a tighter leash on other things – houses, cars, televisions, game systems, or jewelry. Some hoard cold hard cash, building up wealth in investments or real estate. I don't really care a whole lot about big-ticket items, but that doesn't mean I'm off the hook. I can still be a real selfish jerk. If you're not quite ready to concede and embrace that title, however, perhaps you can just admit that everyone at one point or another can be a little selfish. We've all had our Crispito moments, have we not?

I don't think most people are selfish on purpose. Usually we just have some distraction keeping us from seeing the bigger picture. My hunger and excitement kept me from sharing with Jason. Naivety or ignorance can lead us to do some pretty unreasonable stuff, but I don't think it's because we're hard-hearted. We don't understand the needs around us. We don't know how bad some people have it. We aren't mean spirited. We just don't often stop to think about how things really work in this world. If we did, I believe it would change our perspective.

Please know up front that it is my goal in this chapter to completely overwhelm you with the truth. My goal is to shock you into action--to so move you with the truth of how messed up our world is you won't be able to sit still any longer. It's possible you've heard some of these statistics and stories before. Even if you haven't, you probably don't need much convincing that the world is a messed up place.

I threw a question out online to some friends as to how they saw needs in their own lives. I got lots of responses, and quickly. They were all pretty devastating.

There was illiteracy and poor parenting. There was abuse and neglect. There was hatefulness and prejudice. There was poverty and shame. As you read the numbers and the stories and it all starts to sink in, I want you to ask yourself what you are going to do about it.

Phaeton, Haiti is about three feet above sea level and 180 miles north of Port au Prince. The village is home to roughly 2,500 people. You've probably never heard of it. It isn't very noteworthy. I've never been there but my wife has. I remember her telling me about it for the first time, and tears welled up in her eyes as she did so. By far, it's the most poverty stricken place she'd ever visited.

It's twenty kilometers to the nearest market. Only those who can afford a ride there have access to what they offer. The people survive on fish from the sea, fruit from their trees, and diminishing amounts of human willpower. Orange-tinted hair is ubiquitous, a well-known indicator malnourishment. There used to be a rope factory there that employed the town's residents, but it was shuttered years ago. These people now exist in abject poverty. Look around you at the basic utilities you take for granted in your home—electricity, running water, indoor plumbing. These are rare in the village. There are things that happen in this town that don't seem like real life.

My wife told me about seeing a young boy in town hit by a passing motorcycle. He lay stunned and motionless on the ground for a moment as people rushed to help him. There are no ambulances, no hospital, and no paramedics rushing to the scene. A bystander picked the boy up *by his head*, turned him side to side, and then set him down. Apparently this test demonstrated his wellness. Nothing else was done.

I still wonder sometimes what happened to that child. Did he live? Were there internal injuries no one could detect? Where were his parents?

In all the pictures I've ever seen of people in Phaeton, only one included people smiling. It's just not natural to them. It is well documented that Haiti is the poorest nation in the western hemisphere. Seventy-seven percent of its citizens live in poverty. More than half of the population lives on $1 or less.

How do you live on less than a dollar?

While I've never been to Haiti, I've seen this kind of poverty up close, and it was a jarring experience.

In 2005 I visited Santiago, Dominican Republic for the first time. While there, we visited a community known as The Hole. The name is appropriate. Hundreds of people live in a giant hole in the middle of the city, a place that was once the town dump. Pigs lay cooling in the river of filthy water; goats munched on pieces of trash alongside children who are starving.

I wonder if when no Americans are looking the kids nibble on the trash too. While in The Hole we visited a nutrition center that was serving lunch. This was the only meal most of the children would get that day, and they only got it six days each week. A crowd of kids appeared around the center. They were not allowed in. The center couldn't afford to feed everyone. I watched as one kid secretly passed his vitamin through the railing to a friend.

I wondered in horror if the vitamin would be the only thing that settled into the child's stomach that day. Unfortunately, probably so.

That same trip we traveled to another community built at the base of a mountain of garbage in the new trash dump. The gigantic pile of the city's waste was constantly smoldering. When a truck came to drop off more trash, residents scampered up the steep incline to see if anything of value was being discarded.

It was there I met Diana, a little girl of perhaps ten who wore nothing but an oversized t-shirt. Her hair was caked with dust and ash. When she approached our group, I was bent over some concrete mix, sweating in the hot sun. I looked at her and said "Hola." I knew little Spanish, she little English. We exchanged names and then our conversation grinded to a halt. But when she patted her stomach, I knew what she was getting at. She was hungry. I had nothing to offer her and reasoned that I was doing all I could. We were building a nutrition center that would serve her community. Would she be let in? How many kids were in this neighborhood, anyway?

Diana walked away. She was shoeless and still hungry. Now, years later, Diana would be in her late teens. Is she a mother? Did she ever find some shoes? Is she alive?

Poverty is only one way the world is messed up. Unfortunately, many other tragedies persist around the globe. One of them is human trafficking.

In the northeast corner of India, near the border of Nepal and Bhutan and Bangladesh, there is a red light district. Kids there are forced to inhale gasoline to curb their appetite during the day. They, or their mothers, or both, are then forced to service perverted clients all night. Mother and children live in the same room, and even if the kids aren't sold to abusive customers they are often forced to watch as their mothers are ravaged.

In what universe is that okay?

This is not a far-off problem. In Houston, Texas, there is an international district. It is less than thirty minutes from my house. A row of storefronts sits far enough off the main drag it doesn't invite much suspicion. But the dimly lit strip mall houses massage parlors and "Game Rooms." Inside, it is well known; human beings are trafficked for profit and used in disgusting ways by people who pay a fee. There aren't enough cops devoted to fighting this criminal activity to put a stop to it. Furthermore, they know that if they shut down one shop, the pimps will just move the girls to another location and continue their profitable business. Perhaps upstream in the system somewhere there is corruption that enables it. Either way, it's grievous, not just in Houston, but in every major city in the country.

I am growing weary of hearing *every* city claim

to be "one of the largest hubs of human trafficking in the United States." For there to be enough evil in that many places is just awful. Everywhere you look there's pain and suffering and tragedy and despair.

All over the world.

On and on it goes. Stomach-churning injustices. These are only a handful from my own personal experience. There is poverty and hunger and thirst and persecution and perversion and all manner of evil in every country in the world, including our own. There are refugee wives being abused by their husbands in St. Louis. There are homeless people freezing to death in Jackson, Mississippi. There are poor Native Americans in rural South Dakota being propped up by a system that forced them into their desperate way of life in the first place. I have seen all of these situations with my own eyes. I know of these people's plights first hand. The images are burned in my mind. It's not hypothetical to me. It's not hypothetical to you, either. You've seen it.

I have a friend who lived in Germany growing

up. She reports watching out the window one night when she was only seven as an elderly man slopped through the snow-covered trash cans to dig out food for himself and his sick wife.

One couple I know visited Ethiopia where they supported a child through Compassion International. The boy they sponsored lived with his four siblings, his parents, and his grandparents. The large family lived in a one-room mud hut. They had one bed in one room where they cooked, got dressed, and slept. The floor was dirt. They had no bathroom.

I get a little bent out of shape when I have to wait a minute because *both* of my bathrooms are being used. More of the world lives like the family in Ethiopia than lives like me.

I have a good buddy who lives and ministers in inner city St. Louis. He decided to have a bunch of teenagers over to study the Bible. After a couple of meetings this one kid was kind of out of control. He didn't seem interested, he interrupted a lot, and he didn't really participate. Finally my friend told him if he didn't want to be around then he didn't have to come to the study. The kid sulked through the rest of their meeting.

Afterward, they took a walk together. It took about thirty minutes of persistent questioning, but the kid finally opened up and confessed he couldn't follow along because he couldn't read. Can you imagine being a teenager and not being able to read? I don't mean read *well*. I mean read *at all*.

Some may argue the church should not be about helping people with their physical needs. Instead, we should focus on their spiritual needs. But so often, as was the case with this twelve-year-old boy, the unmet physical needs of people hinder their spiritual growth as well.

I'm telling you--this world is a messed up place. It's frustrating how awful it is. It seems like too much. It's too real. I can see the images in my mind as I sit here and type.

The one-legged boy in India who was leaning on a cane and tapping on our bus window with his free hand, pleading with me in Hindi to give him a few rupees. Likely a slave, the money would go to his master. It's possible that the leg was cut off by his captor to elicit greater sympathy and earn greater profits.

The grown man in India who I have personally shaken hands with. He was sold for a bag of rice when he was a child by his parents. What is that? It's overwhelming. Another news story about molestation or rape, another headline about political corruption, another sad story of hate or persecution or child abuse.

There is extreme hunger in our world. Right now, as you read these words, there are people who are munching on bark for lack of a better option. There's a family of six or eight sharing a cup of rice. There's a kid in The Hole digging through the trash, looking for something to wear.

"In this world you will have trouble," Jesus said. He wasn't kidding.

- The United Nations estimates that nearly 2.5 million people from over 120 countries are bought and sold each year. Approximately one million of these people are children.
- In all, there are over 100 million children enslaved worldwide. They are forced to participate in hazardous physical labor, some in the sex trade.
- More than 1,600 children die each and every day because they are drinking dirty

water.

- 1 in 8 people in the world do not have enough to eat.
- 1.3 billion people around the world exist on less than $1.25 a day, the international poverty line.
- In third world countries, more people die from parasites than cancer.
- Daily, over 19,000 kids under the age of five die of preventable causes.
- The average distance a woman or child walks in Africa or South Asia to collect water is 3.7 miles. A five-gallon bucket of water weighs forty pounds.
- 33% of the world's population is considered to be starving.
- Someone in the world dies of hunger every 3.6 seconds

I double-checked all those stats to make sure they were true. Unfortunately, they are. It is maddening. We live in a world where enough food is produced to feed every single person. It doesn't seem logical, much less just, that people should be starving to death. We don't have a production problem; we have a sharing problem. Women should not have to carry forty pounds of water four miles to get a clean drink to their children. Kids should not be forced to suck gasoline fumes into their lungs so they'll be ready to be assaulted at night by wretched, reprehensible individuals.

Take a look around, people. This world is a messed up place. But this isn't news. Hugh Evans, who is the founder of the Global Poverty Project, says, "People don't need to become more aware of poverty--they need to know how to end it." I agree and would apply that truism to a variety of injustices, not just poverty.

These are complicated problems. They aren't easy fixes. To find the stamina to engage problems of this magnitude we must be completely convinced that the injustices are, in fact, unjust. We must be sickened by the harsh realities we observe. We must be indignant that any such thing is happening on our watch. We must be resolute and thick-skinned and unshakeable in our resolve. A determination such as this only comes from a complete unwillingness to let this awful, messed up world continue to be awful and messed up. This determination is forged and refined by staring such things in the eye and admitting they exist, even if it makes us sick inside.

I don't think our problem is that we see the need and ignore it. I think our sin is not slowing down long enough to recognize it exists.

My daughter and I attended her first baseball game when she was barely four years old. We rode the train down to the stadium and enjoyed her first game together, a rite of passage for any St. Louis kid. We did it up right -- hot dogs and popcorn and sodas and all that. We'd watch an inning and then go exploring to keep her interested. We must've walked around the entire stadium three or four times.

We left early to beat the rush. On the way out of the stadium to the train station we came upon some panhandlers set up near our stop. It was the usual crew. There was a saxophone player blaring ballpark favorites on a continuous loop. There were some folks with no particular talent but just as willing to accept donations.

We weren't the only ones leaving. Many others had the same idea to sneak out ahead of the long lines to get on the train and head for the suburbs. My daughter was hanging on one arm, all hopped up on sugar and excitement. I was reveling in the nice day and the shared experience. The occasional roar of the crowd spilled out of the stadium and was loud enough to drown out our immediate surroundings.

There was so much going on I almost missed seeing her.

She was in a wheelchair, slouched over and wrinkled. Her slight frame was easy to accidentally overlook. What caught my eye was that her face was heavily bandaged on one side. It looked unnatural, and it was clear that she was disfigured beneath the bandages. It stopped me in my tracks. We had nearly walked right past her, completely oblivious. Now that we were stopped, though, it would be awkward to not say hi. We had locked eyes. I knelt down on one knee, my daughter by my side, and said hello.

Her name was Fammy, I learned. She was old, homeless, and desperate. I asked her what had happened to her face and she didn't want to say in front of my little girl. She cupped one hand around her toothless mouth and whispered the horrific truth to me semi-privately that she had been shot. What seemed like a quarter of her head, including one eye, had been damaged. Only the layered bandages made her skull look somewhat symmetrical. The woman sitting three feet from me was missing a good portion of her face.

My gut twisted inside me.

I emptied my pockets for Fammy, and I instructed my daughter to shake her hand and say "Nice to meet you." Fammy marveled at my daughter's beauty and no doubt thought of her own children. Who knows where they were and why they weren't caring for their mother. We walked to the train and rode home, the crowd noise and celebratory hoopla now drowned out by grave condition of the human being we had just met.

That night I knelt again, this time at my daughter's bedside. We prayed for Fammy. As I turned to walk out of my daughter's room I realized she had been impacted deeply. I had been, too.

We had nearly walked right past her.

Proverbs 28:27 says,

> "Whoever gives to the poor will not want,
> but he who hides his eyes will get many a
> curse."

I wonder how this verse applies to our modern life. We seldom see a need and just ignore it, though we do that at times. More often we just don't notice the needs that exist. There's too much noise in our lives and too much going on and we're too preoccupied to notice the needs around us.

If you didn't know any of the stats I shared before, it's not because you're a heartless human being; it's because you're a busy human being. If you've never had an encounter like I have with Fammy or the one-legged boy in India or Diana in the Dominican Republic, it's not because you don't care. It's because you're busy doing other stuff. You keep your head down, work hard, and try to believe that your life matters.

This world is too messed up to ignore. The incredible darkness in this life won't make you feel warm and fuzzy, but as a Christ follower, we have no excuse to turn our eyes away. To hide our eyes from the problem does not make the problem disappear; it just keeps it from inconveniencing us.

It was John Bunyan who said, "You have not lived today until you have done something for someone who can never repay you."

You're not going to abolish human trafficking or feed every hungry kid on earth by looking up from your busy life, but you can make an impact. I would encourage every single person reading these words to set aside some time to notice. Get out there and engage with people who have less. Learn someone's name that has been sold like a piece of property. Visit a slum. Volunteer at a homeless shelter. Listen to a story that's hard to listen to.

Recognize what's going on around you. We're not going to be able to let loose of the values that distract and numb us until we see what the world is really like.

Even if it hurts.

———————

Before we moved to Texas a few years ago, I decided to go to one last Cardinals game by myself.

I don't remember why. I had a free pass or something and the rest of my family was busy and I wanted to go eat a foot long bratwurst and see the Redbirds play one more time.

I drove down to the city, parked in a cheap lot, and walked a few blocks over to the stadium. As I walked across an urban plaza, I saw her and couldn't believe my eyes. It was Fammy. She was still in a wheelchair, alone, her face still bandaged but not as heavily. I walked up to her and called her by name. It had been years, but I still remembered.

I would never forget Fammy.

She had found a place to live and was getting by on disability. I think she had reconnected with a son. She looked well, face bandages not withstanding. We only chatted for a moment, and as I walked away I wondered again what would have happened if I had walked passed her that first day outside the stadium.

There are a lot of people like Fammy out there. They are starving and sick and lonely. They are bought and sold like a commodity. They are walking long distances to fetch drinkable water. They are desperate.

They are hopeless.

The world is a messed up place. There's no other way to look at it. It's impossible to ignore.

If we stop to look, that is.

3 | Rich

"Be on your guard against all kinds of greed; life does not consist in an abundance of possessions."
Jesus, Luke 12:15

We need to go back and take a look at that passage from 1 Timothy 6:17-19 again. Remember what it said?

> "Command those who are rich in this present world not to be arrogant nor to put their hope in wealth, which is so uncertain, but to put their hope in God, who richly provides us with everything for our

enjoyment. Command them to do good, to be rich in good deeds, and *to be generous and willing to share.* (Emphasis is mine) In this way they will lay up treasure for themselves as a firm foundation for the coming age, so that they may take hold of the life that is truly life."

Paul writes these words to Timothy, a young church leader he had been mentoring. It was a hard teaching then, and it is a hard teaching now. As you read it, you probably skimmed it real fast and made some conclusions. I know what I always thought about this passage.

"Yeah! Those rich fools need to get with the program and be more generous! We could solve a lot of problems that way!"

I thought this way for the vast majority of my life. Until I realized *I* was rich, that is.

It was a mistake for me to believe that passages like this one were not intended for me. We usually think the financial universe revolves around us. We are the average earner in our minds. Everyone who makes more than us is rich. So passages like this one often go ignored. It's not that we don't *agree* with what it says; it's just that it addresses a group of people to whom we do not believe we belong. It's irrelevant.

It's for rich people, not us.

But if you are reading this book, you are rich. You are *filthy* rich. I am rich. I'm a pastor in my early thirties, and I am in the top 1% of the richest people in the world. We live in a rich nation. We live in rich states. We have rich communities. Even the poorest among us are relatively rich.

The global poverty line is $1.25 a day. The poverty line in American is in the tens of thousands, with cost of living figured in and all that. Still, it costs more to live in a rich nation. So the fact remains—we are rich.

If we can just accept this fact, then this passage takes on new life. It transforms from a teaching for others to a teaching for all of us.

Ultimately we have two options as rich people. We can pat ourselves on the back, surround ourselves with comfort and luxury and delight in our wealth, or we can be generous and willing to share.

The church should be known as the most generous people on the planet. Historically, that's been the case. Even huge philanthropic organizations that aren't overtly Christian now are historically rooted in faith. That's why it's called a Red *Cross* and the *Salvation* Army. But the roots of our collective generosity go much further. The earliest Christians were very generous.

Read Acts 4 and you'll see it's true. At the end of the chapter, we read that there was no one in the church who lacked anything because everyone was willing to share. They didn't consider anything that they had as their own. Some, including Joseph (aka Barnabas) sold some land—in his agrarian culture, this was his very livelihood--and brought it to the apostles to be dispersed as needed.

> "Now Joseph, a Levite of Cyprian birth, who was also called Barnabas by the apostles (which translated means Son of Encouragement), and who owned a tract of land, sold it and brought the money and laid it at the apostles' feet."

Some may argue that the generosity here was directed to the local church, and I can't argue with that. We should take care of our own. I'm using this passage to emphasize the willing spirit of the church to share in general, not attempting to mandate where that generosity be directed particularly. Bottom line: Barnabas was exceedingly generous.

In the very next chapter, we meet Ananias and Sapphira. They also sold some property, but they didn't donate all the money. They kept some back, lied about it, and God struck them both dead. I remember hearing this story for the first time in Jr. High. It was horrifying!

> "But a man named Ananias, with his wife Sapphira, sold a piece of property, and kept back some of the price for himself, with his wife's full knowledge, and bringing a portion of it, he laid it at the apostles' feet. But Peter said, "Ananias, why has Satan filled your heart to lie to the Holy Spirit and to keep back some of the price of the land? While it remained unsold, did it not remain your own? And after it was sold, was it not under your control? Why is it that you have conceived this deed in your heart? You have not lied

to men but to God." And as he heard these words, Ananias fell down and breathed his last; and great fear came over all who heard of it. The young men got up and covered him up and, after carrying him out, buried him.

Now there elapsed an interval of about three hours, and his wife came in, not knowing what had happened. And Peter responded to her, "Tell me whether you sold the land for such and such a price?" And she said, "Yes, that was the price." Then Peter said to her, "Why is it that you have agreed together to put the Spirit of the Lord to the test? Behold, the feet of those who have buried your husband are at the door, and they will carry you out as well." And immediately she fell at his feet and breathed her last, and the young men came in and found her dead, and they carried her out and buried her beside her husband. And great fear came over the whole church, and over all who heard of these things."

Unfortunately, many in the contemporary American church are more like Ananias and Sapphira in Acts 5 than Barnabas in Acts 4. Do you give like Barnabas or do you give like Ananias and Sapphira?

If you're not sure, what follows are some important questions to consider so you can figure it out.

---

1. Do you view your possessions as your possessions?

In Acts 4, they shared everything. The early church gave out of a conviction that everything that they had came from God and belonged to the community. They were so unselfish that they would just share with one another.

In a time when we may be more loyal to our capitalism than we are to Christ, that sounds pretty controversial. For some of you it may sound too liberal, a little bit like socialism. But in the context of the church it's none of those things. The people in Acts 4 were not communists; they were the church. They cared for and provided for one another when there was a need. It was born out of a unity they possessed in every area of their lives. That's not socialism; it's sharing.

"Give to the one who asks you and do not turn away the one who wants to borrow from you." Those are not words from a leading socialist politician--those are the words of Jesus in Matthew 5:42

Do you view your possessions as your possessions and something to cling to? After all, they are *yours*. Or are you willing to loosen your grip and share?

---

2. Do you give to those who have the most need?

Acts 4 says there were no needy people among the church. Not a single one. Isn't that incredible? In a world like ours with so many needs, it's hard to imagine there not being any. But in the early church that was the case.

"The congregation of those who believed

were of one heart and soul. Not one of them claimed that anything belonging to him was his own, but all things were common property to them. And with great power the apostles were giving testimony to the resurrection of the Lord Jesus, and abundant grace was upon them all. For there was not a needy person among them, for all who were owners of land or houses would sell them and bring the proceeds of the sales and lay them at the apostles' feet, and they would be distributed to each as any had need." Acts 4:32-35

Every time there was a need, people rushed to meet it. Do you rush to give to people who need it most?

Jesus says in Matthew 6:2-3,

"So when you give to the poor, do not sound a trumpet before you, as the hypocrites do in the synagogues and in the streets, so that they may be honored by men. Truly I say to you, they have their reward in full. But when you give to the poor, do not let your left hand know what your right hand is doing, so that your giving will be in secret; and your Father who sees what is done in secret will reward you."

Often, that passage is used to instruct us to not be arrogant about our generosity. We should not show off our philanthropy and charity. This is true. (Neither should we use this passage as justification to be secretive about our incomes, spending, and debt load so we don't have to be held accountable for our often-excessive living, but that's another matter entirely.) But the command to not broadcast our generosity is not what strikes me about this passage.

On two occasions, Jesus says "*When* you give you to the needy." Jesus does not say "If." He assumes that giving is going to be a part of how we as rich people act out our faith. He *assumes* that we will be generous with those who have less.

We've already covered the great need that exists in our world in chapter two, so if you slept through that one go back and give it a look. The needs are great. When was the last time you gave to someone who needed it worse than you? If you think dropping a five-dollar bill in the offering plate weekly is going to fix these huge problems, I would beg you to reconsider.

We need to dig deeper. Not just into our pockets, but into our hearts. We are too rich to be satisfied by our token offerings. We are too wealthy to pat ourselves on the back for giving ten percent.

---

3. Does your stinginess rub off on others?

Some of us are just selfish. We worked hard for it, we built it, we earned it, and we don't want to give it away. We dig deep, but it's into ourselves to work harder so we can climb the corporate ladder. We push harder, but it's in the area of effort at work so we have a solid annual review and get a salary bump. We look forward to our next purchase, our new toy. We don't dig deep so we can give more to others; we dig deep so we can earn more for ourselves.

Is that stinginess rubbing off on others? Barnabas was unselfish. His testimony is on the heels of Acts 4 saying this was a common occurrence. He got the idea from watching other people do the same thing. So generosity rubs off. But Luke puts the story of Ananias and Sapphira right beside it. Sadly, selfishness rubs off too.

Sometimes women are more known for being compassionate, generous, and willing to share. Men, there is nothing unmanly about being generous. It is unmanly to put on chap stick, drink from a straw, and watch *The Sound of Music*. If you're a dude, you should avoid these activities whenever possible. My old man never did any of that stuff. My dad is about 6'6", rides a Harley, wears boots, and watches cows being sold on television for fun. No joke. He's a dude.

My whole life, all I watched him do was give. He's one of the most generous people I know. He worked his tail off to make ends meet for our family. He ran farms and put in long hours and just gave and gave of himself.

Sometimes men allow their selfishness to rub off on the rest of their family. We build Kingdoms for ourselves and create in our wives and children an expectation of wanting more and more and more. You've probably heard men complain about being a human ATM, dishing out dollars to their kids who come to them with palms up. But is it possible that they learn that attitude from watching us blow through cash? Men, we set the tone in our families. We need to set a tone of generosity.

---

4. Do you hold back when you give?

Ananias and Sapphira end up dead at the end of this story, but their crime is not being stingy. They gave a whole bunch of money, it seems. They sold something of immense value, and gave *most* of it away. When was the last time you did that?

Their crime was not that they didn't give at all. It's that they held back. They had a heart issue that caused them to appear to give everything, but they didn't.

They held back. They could not loosen their grip on their possessions. Who knows the reason. Probably because they are a lot like us, just with weirder names.

I live near Houston, Texas but I am a bit

fanatical when it comes to the St. Louis Cardinals. Before the Astros defected to the American League, the Cardinals would come to town for a few games each year. I made it a point to get to as many games as I could.

One time my wife and I parked the car and were headed into the stadium when a homeless guy approached us. This is not the first beggar I've ever encountered outside of a professional sports stadium, and I admit to often being suspect. But this guy seemed different. I've heard a lot of speeches from homeless guys. This one was either well rehearsed or not a speech at all. He had a specific amount of money he needed and the purpose was that he needed to get a room that night. He named the place, the location. I had heard of it and the services it offered.

The man needed fifteen bucks.

I talked to the guy, learned his name, and I got into my wallet. Seemed like his story checked out. I was happy to share. I had a ten and a five and some ones. I reached into my wallet, grabbed the ones, handed them to the guy and said "God bless you." Self-congratulatory, I walked away. Pastor – 1, Devil – 0.

We didn't make it ten steps before my wife asked, "You know you had a ten and a five in there. He needed fifteen bucks."

I was busted, but she was right. I was holding back. Pastor – 0, Wife – 1.

I retraced my steps, found the guy, and apologized to him for my selfishness. I gave him the fifteen bucks without asking for the singles back.

The moral of the story is not that I'm generous, but that I'm an idiot. I trick myself into thinking I'm so great because I gave *something* when the truth is I could give *more*. I am rich. So are you. And our best reason to not give is that we simply don't feel like it. We may come up with other reasons-- excuses born out of experience or politics or some other factor--but the truth is we're just selfish. We just don't want to do more. We are too busy clutching our wealth. Our hands are full.

Paul's instruction to Timothy is to tell wealthy people to be generous and willing to share. I need to remind myself of those words.

---

5. How will your selfishness cost you?

Ananias and Sapphira's bones are rotting

because of their deceit and selfishness. They dropped dead instantly upon having their sin uncovered. That may not happen to you the next time you hold back something. I wonder how generous folks would be if that still happened each time someone was stingy. Imagine the offering plates getting passed row by row in church and the crowd just keeling over one by one. Offerings would probably spike dramatically in churches all over the country. The author would most certainly be among the deceased.

Through the story of Ananias and Sapphira, as well as other places, the Scriptures are clear that your selfishness will cost you something.

So often we think to ourselves that we're being wise by holding back, saving some for a rainy day, and building up our personal wealth. This may be controversial, but it's worth noting—the Bible says very little about saving. The few verses that do mention it contrast saving with wasteful spending or as an argument against laziness. When saving and giving go head to head in the Bible, giving always wins. By contrast, it says much about giving.

We have bought into the lie that if we accumulate and accumulate and accumulate we'll be happier, more secure, and better off. We have bought into the lie that we're not rich, that only people who make more than us are rich. Remember Paul's words in 1 Timothy?

"Instruct those who are rich in this present world not to be conceited or to fix their hope on the uncertainty of riches..."

Whether it's the financial crisis of 2008, the Great Depression, the boom and subsequent bust of a particular industry, or a devastating round of layoffs, we've seen the news stories. We've heard of professional athletes who made millions only to declare bankruptcy in retirement. Money can supply us with a lot of things, but it is too fickle to place our hope in.

So why use it to build a Kingdom of our own when we can invest it into God's Kingdom?

We can blame poverty on God. We can blame poverty on bad governance. But the reality is, the reason there are so many needy people is because we don't feel like giving more. We give a little and we pat ourselves on the back for it. The average American gives away less than 5% of their income annually. This bare-minimum selfishness is chiefly responsible for the perpetuation of all that messed up stuff we talked about earlier.

I live in one of the fastest growing, most idyllic regions in the entire United States. The average income in our county is $126,000. Some make less, some make more, but that's the average. Everyone who earns that much is among the top 0.07% of the richest people on earth. It would take the average laborer in Ghana 787 years to earn what a resident of Fort Bend County, Texas makes in a single year.

What if we as the rich decided to heed Paul's words and invest more in "the life that is truly life?" If every resident in Fort Bend County were generous and willing to share, donating 10% of their earnings annually, 7.5 billion dollars would be generated to fund Kingdom work each year. That means every single person around the world living on a dollar a day could then make $7.50 a day. That's just in one county!

What if all us rich folks gave away half our income? We don't have to be all Acts 4 about it and give away *everything*. What if we gave away just half and figured out a way to survive on what was left? Using my community as an example, the average earner would still be among the 0.17% richest people on earth. Even after giving away *half their income,* we would still be in the two-tenths of a percent of the richest people on the planet. Additionally, and shockingly, we would also generate enough new funds to sponsor every child cared for by Compassion International for 65 years.

Again, that's just from one county in Texas.

Imagine the impact of an entire church culture that surrendered to the reality that they are rich and they are called to share. Imagine if we all lived like Barnabas instead of Ananias and Sapphira. Imagine if we let loose of what we held so dear and dug a little deeper to give.

What kind of life are you living? Are you living a life that revolves around yourself? Are you living a life that worships your wealth? Are you living a life that trusts in your money? Don't put your hope in wealth.

Be generous and willing to share.

4 | Idle Worship

"But if anyone has the world's goods and sees his brother in need, yet closes his heart against him, how does God's love abide in him? Little children, let us not love in word or talk but in deed and in truth." 1 John 3:17-18

It was a 1991 Toyota Tercel, and it was all mine. Mine and Dent County Bank's, that is. Purchased from Heavin Motors in Salem, Missouri, I drove it and my new monthly payment off the lot with the excitement of a seventeen year old who had just experienced a serious upgrade.

My previous wheels were ones I shared with my

parents. The 1977 Chevy Monte Carlo that my folks owned was at my disposal on occasion. A 1977 Chevy Monte Carlo was really cool in 1977. Not so much in 1998.

It had a vinyl top that was weathered and cracked, and the paint job was showing it's age. That thing was the length of a small yacht--with an eight-track player and a little button on the floor you pushed to brighten your headlights.

A car is a car, and I drove it gratefully. Still, pulling off the lot with a set of wheels that was less than ten years old made me feel like a million bucks.

The only hindrance to my complete freedom of the road was that the Tercel was a standard transmission. I had driven a "stick" before, but this one was not geared the same as the old pickups I'd maneuvered through hay fields in the summer. It was pretty touchy. The clutch was more responsive than what I was used to. I realized quickly it was not going to be easy to get this car home.

I went around the block, my dad offering encouragement in the passenger seat. We arrived at a stop sign, and my worst nightmare began to unfold. Actually, my worst nightmare is a big furry spider riding a cobra straight toward me while I'm in a dark, closed in space way up in the air, threatening to force-feed me mayonnaise. But I digress.

After looking each way and watching the four-way intersection clear out, I began to release the clutch and press down on the gas. My new car lurched forward suddenly and then came to a dead stop. The motor quit.

I had killed it.

I pressed down on the clutch quickly and started it back up. Eager to get across the street with the intersection still clear, I attempted to take off again. For a second time I was unsuccessful, killing it again. I felt a cool drop of sweat (and by "cool drop of sweat" I mean "my forehead looked like Niagara Falls") begin to form on my brow.

"Give it another try," my dad said.

I realized for the first time that the stop sign I was stalled at was situated on a slight incline. I had done fine on flat surfaces. This was new territory. Each time I pressed down on the clutch my car began to creep backward slightly. I applied the brake because another car had appeared behind me. I now had an audience. For the moment they were waiting patiently.

I would test their patience.

On probably eight to ten occasions, I repeated the embarrassing ritual. I applied the brake to keep from backing into the *line of cars* forming behind me. I then removed my foot from the brake and immediately accelerated with growing desperation. My new car let out a terrible squeal, sensing my intent. But the mechanics wouldn't allow it. My intentions made no difference. Time after time after time, I created a huge batch of noise, but my car went nowhere.

My dad was losing patience, as were the other drivers around me. Once a willing tutor, my old man reached his arm out the window and started waving cars around. Passers by looked in, shaking their heads.

Rookie.

I was hot with nerves. Would I have to switch spots with my dad just to get home? Would I have to push my new car across the intersection? Would we have to turn around and take it back?

I focused as much as I could and started my car back up. With my left foot on the clutch and my right foot on the brake, we waited once more until the coast was clear. With no cars in sight, I took my foot off the brake and began to press on the gas. My angst caused me to apply more pressure than necessary.

The motor of my brand new car revved up and let out an awful sound. It sounded like a kid screaming for help or a drowning victim gasping for air. I let up on the clutch gradually, and it began to lunge forward in what seemed like five-foot increments. It was like I was riding an indecisive bunny rabbit that would stop and go without much consideration of what it would do next. The engine screeched and strained and made wild, desperate sounds. My tires squealed against the asphalt. The noises all joined together and gave me hope that this would be the time of my victory.

Not so.

After a few more lunges and the deafening sounds of my motor attempting to do what I said, my car fell flat. I had been at the intersection for what seemed like an hour. I had created an amazing amount of noise, left a good bit of fumes in my wake, and inconvenienced the lives of many other people. But when it was all said and done, I had barely moved an inch. My new car had strained and stalled out and been started up again.

The only thing it hadn't done is what a car is intended to do.

———————

I tell you this story about my car because I'm afraid that sometimes that's how the church operates. We make a lot of noise. We leave a lot of fumes in our wake. People know we're there, if for no other reason than we are loud or in their way.

But far too often, I'm afraid, we are idle worshippers.

Idol worship is condemned in the Scripture and in the life of the contemporary church. *Idle* worship is condemned by the Scriptures but often is embraced by the contemporary church. Those of us who would never bow before an altar built in honor of another god bow often before the god of our comfort.

Sing? Oh, we can sing loudly. The church now has an entire industry devoted to producing and selling worship music. Revenue in this industry is over a billion dollars annually. I'm not saying singing to God is bad. There are plenty of passages in the Bible where we are instructed to raise our voices to God in song.

We're just not supposed to do it to the neglect of justice and generosity and helping the poor. If we sing but don't do what God says, we're only making noise. We're like my car--lurching and moaning and threatening to move, but remaining still.

Pastor and author David Platt puts it this way:

"I am convinced that we as Christ followers in American churches have embraced values and ideas that are not only unbiblical but that actually contradict the gospel we claim to believe."

If we value the worship experience more highly than we value looking out for the marginalized, we misunderstand what worship is. If we serve ourselves more than we serve the outcast, we misunderstand what it actually means to serve. If we make a lot of noise and run a lot of programs and generate a lot of buzz more than we engage with the hurting people around us, we have forgotten why it is we exist as the people of God. At the church where I serve we have three values – *Move Toward, Move Forward,* and *Move Outward.* It's that third one that I'm talking about here. If you're church isn't living out that value, then you really have to ask what it is your church is doing at all.

This is not a new challenge. God's people have been lunging and squealing for centuries, and I fear the church is guilty of the same loud inactivity these days. The Old Testament is full of prophetic warnings concerning the customs, traditions, and rituals of God's people.

Isaiah records the Lord's judgment against His own people in Isaiah 3:13-15:

> "The Lord arises to contend, and stands to judge the people. The Lord enters into judgment with the elders and princes of His people, 'It is you who have devoured the vineyard; The plunder of the poor is in your houses. What do you mean by crushing My peopleand grinding the face of the poor,'declares the Lord God of hosts."

His judgment, the passage concludes, is physical and spiritual torment. They will be branded by their captors, mourn at their gates, and have their lives lost in battle.

You can almost hear God's frustration. "How dare you oppress the poor. What do you mean you crush the poor? What's up with that!"?

Jeremiah beats the same drum:

> "They are fat, they are sleek, they also excel in deeds of wickedness; they do not plead the cause of the orphan...they do not defend the rights of the poor. Shall I not punish these people? On a nation such as this shall I not avenge myself?" (Jeremiah 5:28-29)

Of all the prophets, Amos has the most to say on the subject.

The prophet Amos was a shepherd. He bursts on the scene with a blunt critique of many godless nations, Israel included. In Amos 4:1 he says,

> "Hear this word, you cows of Bashan who are on the mountain of Samaria, who oppress the poor, who crush the needy, who say to your husbands, 'Bring now, that we may drink!' The Lord God has sworn by His

holiness, 'Behold, the days are coming upon you when they will take you away with meat hooks and the last of you with fish hooks."

God calls them self-indulgent cows and swears they will be led into slavery with fishhooks through their mouths. Because of their injustice, the people of God will be judged ever so severely.

The crazy part of all this is these are not the enemies of God receiving these messages of judgment. They are the people of God. They govern the temple and offer sacrifices and commemorate festivals in accordance with the law. They worship exactly how they were instructed. They sing and dance and celebrate. The problem is, as is abundantly clear, God doesn't care how much noise they generate.

He wants them to *do* something. My car did everything except what a car was supposed to do. May that never be said of the church!

In Amos 5:21-23, the prophet speaks on God's behalf regarding all the songs the people would sing:

"I hate, I reject your festivals, nor do I

delight in your solemn assemblies. Even though you offer up to Me burnt offerings and your grain offerings, I will not accept them; And I will not even look at the peace offerings of your fatlings. Take away from Me the noise of your songs; I will not even listen to the sound of your harps."

1 Samuel 15:22 says, "to obey is better than sacrifice." In Hosea 6:6 God asserts, "I desire mercy, not sacrifice."

The sacrificial system was a method of worship that involved much process and ritual, as do our modern methods of singing and communion and special events. Our concerts and programs and sermons generate much enthusiasm and keep folks busy doing good things. Make no mistake, they *are* good things.

But absent from justice and mercy and love and actually doing something in Jesus' name for Jesus' people, they are all meaningless. According to the prophets, God doesn't even want to hear it. And if our celebrations continue at the cost of serving the poor, God will judge us for our inactivity.

Amos 8 says that God will not forget those who trample the needy. Instead, He will judge them harshly. "They will fall and not rise again" (Amos 8:14).

What are we supposed to make of all this? Did God really feel that strongly about how the poor are treated? Does He still? The New Testament paints a picture of a God who is extremely concerned with the poor. Jesus says, "Blessed are you who are poor, for yours is the Kingdom of God" (Luke 6:20) He also seems a little preoccupied with warning the rich who may grow idle in their abundance. Just a few verses later Jesus says, "Woe to you who are rich, for you are receiving your comfort in full" (Luke 6:25)

James, the brother of Jesus, says much about the condition of the poor among us. In James 2:5 he urges us not to show favoritism to the wealthy, arguing, "did not God choose the poor of this world to be rich in faith and heirs of the kingdom which He promised to those who love Him?"

The nation of Israel was judged harshly because they sang and sacrificed and put on a big show, but they neglected the needy and lived in comfort and luxury. They did all the things they thought they were supposed to do to honor God. But they forgot the poor, and they were judged harshly for it.

Most churches do so much that it leaves little margin to engage with the poor in meaningful ways. Often we give our money, but we're not willing to give our time. For marginalized people in our communities and around the globe, the Church is supposed to be a place where they can turn for help. With all the programs, big event outreaches, small group Bible studies, social gatherings, sports leagues, retreats and other things that we do, is it possible that all that noise keeps us too busy to live out our true purpose?

Is it possible that we need to let loose of some of that stuff so we can take hold of the mission to love and serve the needy among us?

If we are supposed to be among the most generous people on the face of the earth, what do we need to stop doing so we can start doing more to combat injustice? More to the point, are we even *willing* to stop doing other good things so we don't neglect those in need?

If God sent prophets to our churches today, in small towns across the Midwest and in affluent suburban communities like the one where I live, would their message be much different from the message brought by Isaiah, Jeremiah, and Amos?

———————

I finally got my car across that intersection. After all the lunging and sweat and backed up traffic and testing my dad's patience to the very end, I figured out the right amount of clutch to go with the right amount of gas. I didn't want to cause a scene and make a big mess out of things.

First gear is often the hardest to find. Once I got across the street, I had no trouble picking up speed and shifting from gear to gear. I believe the same is possible for the church. What we face is not an insurmountable task. We just have some thinking and maybe some reprioritizing to do. I believe the church in America believes it loves God. I believe the church in America believes it loves those around the world who so often go without basic human needs.

But the true test of our affection is not found in our elaborate buildings and our slick programs and our glossy literature. It's found in our refusal to let the good things we do be an excuse that keeps us from obeying Jesus' words to care about the poor and oppressed.

As 1 John says, our love needs to be evident not just in what we say (or sing), but in how we live:

> *"But if anyone has the world's goods and sees his brother in need, yet closes his heart against him, how does God's love abide in him? Little children, let us not love in word or talk but in deed and in truth." 1 John 3:17-18*

5 | Excuses

If a brother or sister is poorly clothed and lacking in daily food, and one of you says to them, "Go in peace, be warmed and filled," without giving them the things needed for the body, what good is that?" James 2:15-16

He held a cardboard sign tightly to keep it flapping from the gusting wind. Scraggly beard, tattered clothing, glazed-over look in his eye, the man at the stop light almost looked scripted. I don't know if he was high or just exhausted. The sign he held was pretty straightforward:

"Need sixty cents for a bus ticket."

I emptied the change out of my minivan's ashtray and wished the man "God bless you." There had to have been at least a buck-fifty in coins in there. Get you a soda while you're at it, fella. It's no trouble.

As the willing, pious poster child of generosity, I continued on my way. Just another day of storing up those treasures in heaven. Nothing to see here. I could almost envision the man purchasing his bus ticket, thanks to my generosity. He would probably be boarding the silver eagle for the long ride home before noon and enjoying a sweet reunion with his family by supper. Tears flowing, they would sit down to a bountiful feast. All the wrongs were forgiven. A fire was lit in the fireplace. I had orchestrated it all with my magnanimous donation. Patting myself on the back once more, I went on about my day. As you can probably tell by now, I can be a very smug giver.

Less than 24 hours later I returned to the same intersection. To my surprise, the same old man was standing there with the same sign in hand. "Need sixty cents for a bus ticket." I was a couple lanes over from the median where he stood, but I still had to suppress the urge to roll down my window and give that guy a piece of my mind. After my self-congratulatory provision the day before, I *knew* he had enough for his alleged purchase. Why was he still standing there? And if he was just ripping people off, couldn't he muster up the creativity to make a new sign? Or rotate to a different intersection? It was all just sadly obvious.

I had been deceived, and I didn't like it one bit.

My guess is you've had a similar experience. Seeing things like that is reason enough for some people to never give out another dime. In a world as messed up as the one we live in, even kindness is corrupted sometimes. That someone would abuse our generosity is a popular excuse we use to not give.

But it's not our only excuse.

In fact, we have lots of reasons why we won't share. Some sound noble or even spiritual. In this chapter, I would like to obliterate each of them, but not as a means of condemning anyone. In fact, I've said or thought many of the excuses I'll deconstruct. My hope, rather, is to encourage you to dig deeper. I want us to think harder about our motivations and about the excuses we often employ to free us from the act of giving. If you're anything like me, there's more to it than the seemingly spiritual words we say. Often our excuses expose a heart problem on our part.

You may not agree with me as you read this chapter, but I hope you'll think it through with an open mind as you examine your own willingness to give.

———

"They might buy drugs with it."

This is the most popular excuse to not give out money, especially in situations like the one I listed above. The beggar on the street is a stranger. We know nothing about him or her. Our first encounter is a request for money and nothing more. How can we trust them? How can we be sure they won't use our funds for evil?

The truth is, they might really buy dope with the money you give them, and that thought paralyzes us. We'd hate to enable their sin. Moreover, we consider it a bad steward of God's money to give it to someone who will use it for something bad. Kind of like playing the lottery.

The problem with this excuse is two-fold.

First, we can't abide helping someone else sin; yet we're sinning by being judgmental and assuming they're up to no good. Do you think in the history of panhandling there has even been someone who actually spent the funds they collected to buy food? Probably so. Not every homeless person is on drugs. Some folks actually want to buy a can of beans or a bottle of water. It's a little judgmental of us to assume the worst every time.

Second, our attitude lacks quite a bit of creativity in assuming that the only way we can bless those folks is by giving them money. My church does this cool thing called blessing bags. We collect a bunch of stuff—granola bars, bottled water, toothpaste— and put it all in gallon sized plastic bags. Then we distribute them to our congregation so that in a situation like the one I described above, we've got something to offer someone in need.

Thirdly, we don't apply this logic consistently in our lives. There are *lots* of people we give our money to who do bad things with it. We buy sugar harvested on the backs of slave laborers, for instance, without giving it a second thought.

"God helps those who help themselves."

This excuse is also known as, *"The Bible says* 'God helps those who help themselves.'" Incidentally, the Bible *does not* say anything of the sort, but that doesn't stop some of us from using this quip as justification for not sharing.

Some people would point to 2 Thessalonians 3:10 which states, "If anyone is not willing to work, then he is not to eat either." I certainly agree that people should be willing to work for provision. But we shouldn't let that verse inform every instance of generosity. The truth is, in a world as complicated as ours, there are plenty of people who can't get a job for one reason or another.

How exactly do you expect the four-year-old boy in Africa who has AIDS and no clean source of drinking water to "help himself?" What precisely does a woman who lost her entire family to genocide do to get a leg up in a male-dominated country where unemployment is over thirty percent and she lives in a village of a couple hundred people?

I get that if someone is able to work, they should work. Most of the time this isn't the need before us. Certainly it's not true worldwide. There are a lot of people in our global neighborhood who *cannot* help themselves.

God is all about helping those who *cannot* help themselves. Take another flip through the Scriptures. We are without hope in this world if not for Christ and His redeeming work. God saw fit to rescue us. We should be about redemption, too.

"I already gave to _____."

Fill in the blank. I'm sure you're a generous person. You likely give to many causes. Sometimes we think that by giving once (or twice, or three times) we abdicate ourselves from any future obligation. Maybe you give to your church so you don't think it is necessary to sponsor a child who is starving to death. Or maybe you bought a magazine from a kid who came by door to door in your neighborhood. You feel like a pretty generous person. How much are you supposed to give, anyway? Let's not get carried away!

Two thoughts on this.

First, buying Girl Scout cookies isn't exactly the same as helping those who are dying of starvation. Don't get me wrong—I love a good Girl Scout cookie. Thin Mints, Somoas, Shortbread—I'm not a distinguisher of cookies. I'll eat them all. At once. Raise your hand if you are now craving a Girl Scout cookie. I am raising my hand. But me forking over some money to support my local troop does not mean I don't have an obligation to my brothers and sisters who are starving to death.

Secondly, where did we get the idea that there is a maximum amount we're called to give and that once reached, we no longer have to give any more? I can't find it in the Bible, and I don't think it makes much sense. And if you're thinking that a tithe (or 10%) is what the Bible commands, think again. It is sacrifice that is called for in the New Testament Scriptures, not a percentage commitment. Tithing is a start, not where we max out. If you don't want to take my word for it, read 2 Corinthians 8. Only read it if you're ready to be challenged deeply. It makes plain there should be no maximum limit to our generosity. In addition, and uncomfortably for those who don't like the politically charged topic of income redistribution, it sets equality as the goal among believers. No joke. 2 Corinthians 8:14. Check it out.

In Mark 12 Jesus teaches His disciples about giving, using a widow woman's sacrificial offering as an example. After many wealthy folks plopped their large sums of money into the collection plate, this poor widow contributes two small copper coins. Jesus turns to the disciples and says,

> "Truly I say to you this poor widow has put in more than all those who are contributing...for they all contributed out of their abundance, but she out of her poverty has put in everything she had, all she had to live on." (Mark 12:43-44)

One last thought on this excuse: Why is it that we ask the question, "How much does God want me to give?" instead of "How much does God want me to keep?"

"They're just pretending. They make good money doing that! How do we even know they're for real?"

This is another popular one when we encounter someone on the street. It's also a cynicism that creeps in when we hear of corruption among nonprofit organizations or ministries that profit off the sympathies of generous people.

The truth is, you don't know if they are telling you a story or not. But that's not the point. We are smart enough to do due diligence if it's an organization asking us for money. If it's a person on the street, that's more difficult. But if they earn a living lying to everyone about their life, what is it to you? The point we cannot overlook is *are we willing to share* or not. Sometimes our cynicism is a cover-up for our selfishness. If they're a faker, that's on them. If you're selfish and stingy and unwilling to share, that's on you.

"There are government programs for that."

This is one of my favorites. By "favorites" I mean "absolute least favorites."

I can be pretty cynical about government, and I'm not the only one. The track record of government accomplishments in my lifetime is not lengthy or inspiring. Some are extra critical of government for attempting to do more for the poor and seeking more equality in the population of our country.

In some ways, I agree. While there is a great need, the process can be wasteful. It enables folks to depend on the system. Anyone can see the flaws. The federal government shouldn't spend that much money passing out benefits to those in need. But my quarrel is not with the government, actually.

What frustrates me is that most churches don't seem to make an effort to solve the problem themselves. I am honored to serve at a church that really does care about serving our community, both near us and around the world. But benevolent work is sparse in most churches. Even those congregations with leaders who try to do more are often underfunded by their people.

Perhaps if the church in America and elsewhere amped up our efforts to assist those in need we would not see the cycle of poverty perpetuated in so many communities around the world.

The reason I think the Church could actually break this cycle is because we don't just funnel money towards problems but we link arms with neighborhoods through relationships, bringing with us the hope of the Gospel.

We can critique the government or we can depend on the government in regards to helping the poor. But it is unfair for us to do both. If we don't like how they're handling it, let's step up to bad and do better.

"I have given and given and they aren't changing their ways."

This and other excuses like it expose a flaw in our motivation. Often you and I give with strings attached. If we do this, we expect some result. We expect people to be appreciative. We expect them to get their act together. If what we expect doesn't come to pass, we terminate our willingness to be helpful. It's like an investment we make in a stock— if it doesn't mature, we dump it.

Ken Solts said, "Generosity is not always tax deductible." What I think he's getting at there is that there is not always a payoff for us when dishing out kindness. Sometimes people will let us down.

We should be kind and benevolent anyway.

"They need to learn to figure it out."

Figure what out? How do you beat an addiction when the drugs are the only things that distract you from your overwhelming hunger? How do you get a job when you can't afford a decent pair of shoes, and how do you afford a decent pair of shoes when you don't have a job? And how do you folks figure it out when they can't even get the dudes in their cars to roll down their window and learn their name and their story. We all just drive by, eyes forward, pretending like they don't exist. We pick up our phones and press them to our ear so the panhandler will pass us by. To my shame, I admit to having done this.

"They need to learn to figure it out?" Please, if you've ever used this excuse, don't ever use it again. You commit to that, and I'll commit to leaving my cell phone in the cup holder.

"They need to hit rock bottom."

Easy for you to say. I would say that standing on a street corner with a sign made out of scrap paper begging for money *is* rock bottom, but that's just me.

Being an alcoholic with no healthcare, job, or house seems like rock bottom. Walking a 5k to get to a source of clean drinking water seems like rock bottom to me. So does living on a $1 a day or less. Sure, desperation can change our perspective in life and increase our motivation at times. It can also cause us to lose hope completely. Should we really wait until someone is about to give up before we're willing to help? Why would we think that?

Is it because we have a Messiah complex and prefer to come in and save the day so we have a better story to tell our friends? Or are we just cruel, only willing to be inconvenienced if absolutely necessary.

When all the other excuses fall short, we offer up a couple of Bible excuses. These not only sound completely justifiable, they have the added benefit of sounding really spiritual, too. If we examine them more closely, however, we find that they don't hold much water.

Here are the two most common spiritual excuses we use to not let loose of our stuff and be generous:

"Jesus said, 'The poor you will always have with you."

Jesus says this, for sure. A woman brings out some pricey perfume and uses it to anoint Jesus for burial a few days before He dies. The Scripture in question here is Matthew 26:11 if you want to look it up. Modern day believers seek to utilize Jesus' words to support the thesis that social justice is not that big of a deal. The poor will always be around, so why prioritize serving them? We need to just focus on Jesus like the woman does. The problem is, we completely misunderstand the passage to interpret it this way. When you read whole story (and this event is recorded in all four Gospels, which says something of it's importance) we get a more complete meaning of Jesus' words.

For one thing, Jesus says it *in response to the disciples' attitude.* They thought the woman pouring expensive perfume on Him was a little wasteful. Let that sink in. They thought her being so generous was wasteful. In the parallel passage in John 12, we learn that Judas pioneered this critical attitude, not because he wanted to help the poor but because he had sticky fingers and stole from the collection the disciples kept on hand. So if you want to use this reasoning to not give, just remember the company you're in.

Secondly, the full response Jesus gives can be found in Mark 14:6-7. There, when the disciples express their displeasure at this lavish action, we get a little different sense of what he's saying.

> "Let her alone; why do you bother her? She has done a good deed to me. For you will always have the poor with you, *and whenever you wish you can do good to them;* but you do not always have me."

The emphasis is of course mine, but I italicize it to make a point. In no way is Jesus saying that, "Hey, there will always be poor people, so don't bother helping them. I mean, it's not going to do any good." The opposite seems true. Indeed, it sounds like Jesus is saying we *should* help the needy, that their very presence among us serves as our mandate. In this case, though, he welcomes the woman's act of worship and rebuffs the disciples' selfish attitude.

So let's knock it off with the "There-will-always-be-poor-people-Jesus-said-it-so-why-bother" nonsense. The existence of poor people is not a reason not to loosen our grip on what is "ours." Rather, it is a reminder of the work we are supposed to be about.

Moreover, Jesus is actually quoting Deuteronomy 15:11 here. He only says the first part, but in a Jewish audience that likely had the Torah memorized, the latter part was surely brought to mind. Like us remembering a favorite song when we hear just a few of the words. Here's what Deuteronomy 15:11 says:

"For there will never cease to be poor in

the land. Therefore I command you, 'You
shall open wide your hand to your brother,
to the needy and to the poor, in your
land.'"

Jesus is the object of our worship. On that we
can agree. But the object of our worship is telling us
to engage with the least of these every chance we
get.

**"Jesus didn't come to help the poor. He
came to save sinners."**

This is an equally popular excuse, and frankly
the hardest to refute. It's difficult to argue because
Jesus did come to save sinners. Our God
condescended to us to rescue us from Satan, sin,
and death. That was His mission. Jesus Himself
said that He came to seek and save that which was
lost (Luke 19:10). The irony for folks that use this
excuse to not be generous is that Jesus says this on
the heels of Zaccheus' conversion when he commits
to giving half his personal wealth to the poor. Upon
making this financial commitment, Jesus responds

that salvation has come to his house.

I'm not suggesting that if you give away half your stuff you're automatically saved. Nor am I suggesting that Zaccheus was saved by anything other than the grace of Jesus Christ. His work of generosity is not what rescued him from hell. Only the grace of God can save.

What I am saying is that generosity is a normal response to the salvation that we do experience through Christ. His great generosity to us inspires us to live the same way—with our money, with our time, with our love. Jesus commands it elsewhere, and He commends it here. Zaccheus has done a good thing in response to the good things Jesus has done in His life.

I also find it interesting that we attempt to pigeonhole Jesus into only being about one thing. To say He was about saving sinners is true. But must He *only* be about that?

In Luke 4 Jesus' public ministry begins. Fresh off the temptation in the wilderness, He sits down in the synagogue of His hometown to teach. Here's what He says:

"The Spirit of the Lord is upon me,

because He anointed me to preach the Gospel to the poor. He has sent me to proclaim the release to the captives, and recovery of sight to the blind, to set free those who are oppressed, to proclaim the favorable year of the Lord" (Luke 4:18-19).

So in announcing what His work is going to be about, Jesus says four things—he's going to preach the Gospel to the poor, release the captives, give sight to the blind, and set free the oppressed. Some may try to argue that He meant all four in symbolic, spiritual ways. I simply disagree.

Jesus was here to save sinners. He was here to save sinners *and* help the poor, and I think that's what we should be about too.

———————

Whatever excuses you may have used in the past to justify not giving to those in need, I hope you'll reconsider your position. The truth is, there is no excuse to be selfish. Whether in the Old Testament or New, the constant refrain from God to His people is that we would have an unclenched fist and a willing heart to share.

6 | Money

"For the love of money is a root of all kinds of evils. It is through this craving that some have wandered away from the faith and pierced themselves with many pangs." 1 Timothy 6:10

Money isn't evil; it's a tool.

I know that I've been going on and on about how there's injustice and inequality and God calls us to serve the poor and needy. The danger as we think on these things is that we would feel guilty for what we have and think that being rich is evil. The Bible says no such thing.

Nowhere in the Scripture do we read that being

rich wins you an all-expense trip to what as a kid I knew as the "downstairs place." Jesus never condemns anyone for making money. There's not a single verse that equates having possessions with eternal punishment.

So if money isn't bad, then what is it?

Let's revisit 1 Timothy 6:17-19 for some clues.

> "As for the rich in this present age, charge them not to be haughty, nor to set their hopes on the uncertainty of riches, but on God, who richly provides us with everything to enjoy. They are to do good, to be rich in good works, to be generous and ready to share, thus storing up treasure for themselves as a good foundation for the future, so that they may take hold of that which is truly life."

I draw two obvious conclusions from that text. I know really smart Bible folks could unearth more meaning, but there are two things I notice right off the bat.

For one thing, money is dangerous. There is something about money when entrusted to the care of a human being that makes it an explosive thing. Though neutral in and of itself, money can be misused by corrupt individuals and systems when in the hands of fallen humanity.

That's why Paul urges Timothy to instruct folks not to let their riches make them arrogant. He also warns them to not put their hope in the uncertainty of their riches. It's just too shaky of a foundation to build a life on.

Money causes people to manipulate, lie, grow greedy, and become disillusioned. Money can take people captive and enslave them. It can become an idol.

Jesus says as much after His encounter with the Rich Young Man. In Matthew 19, this apparently devout fellow comes to Jesus and asks what he needs to do to get eternal life. My wife pointed out to me one time that she thought it was interesting he did *not* ask what it would take to follow Jesus; he just wanted to know how to get to heaven. My wife is pretty smart and I found that interesting too. Already the guy was out of line. He wanted salvation, not lordship. But that's another matter.

After a little dialogue, Jesus finally says to this guy that he needs to sell all his stuff and follow

Him. Famously, the guy walks away sad because "he had great possessions." As the dude walks away with his tail between his legs, Jesus turns to His disciples and says, "Truly I say to you, only with difficulty will a rich person enter the Kingdom of heaven."

The lesson we learn is that money may not earn you a ticket to hell, but it doesn't earn you a ticket to heaven either.

———————

More than being dangerous, money is a tool. There are lots of tools that are dangerous. We understand this. That's why we wear special masks when we weld and don't let our children operate table saws. To keep a tool from killing us, we take care to use it the way it is intended.

Understanding what the Bible says about money is important if we're going to avoid hurting ourselves with it. Most of the damage we see around us that is caused by money is because people are misusing it in some way.

When it's invested in Kingdom work, which is how Paul suggests to Timothy it should be utilized;

it can provide a great foundation for the future. By being rich in good works, being generous, and being ready to share, the wealthy can take their blessings and use them to be a blessing to others.

Where many folks get off track is that they are building the wrong kingdom with their resources. Instead of building God's Kingdom, they are building up their own.

Just a few verses before Paul's instruction to Timothy on how to coach the rich toward good deeds and generosity, Paul says something else noteworthy.

He famously advises,

> "The love of money is a root of all kinds of evils. It is through this craving that some have wandered away from the faith and pierced themselves with many pangs" (1 Timothy 6:10).

Paul describes a misuse of the tool of money here, declaring that loving our wealth is a sure sign that we're wandering from faith and doing ourselves harm.

Strangely enough, this passage is used to defend

the love of money. People quote it and declare that the Bible never says money is bad, just that the *love of money* is wrong. True enough. But it begs an important question—one we often don't even bother to ask.

How do we know if we love money?

To answer that question, we must look at the verses that precede this one.

> "But godliness with contentment is great gain, for we brought nothing into the world, and we cannot take anything out of the world. But if we have food and clothing, with these we will be content. But those who desire to be rich fall into temptation, into a snare, into many senseless and harmful desires that plunge people into ruin and destruction. For the love of money is a root of all kinds of evils. It is through this craving that some have wandered away from the faith and pierced themselves with many pangs." (I Timothy 6:6-10)

Taken as a whole, this passage seems to give us a

key indicator of a love for money in our lives. It's mentioned three or four times in this text. If you want to know whether or not you love money, whether or not your grip on your stuff is too tight, whether or not you are misusing the tool that God has blessed you with, this is the question you need to ask yourself. Better yet, ask your spouse or best friend this question:

Are you content?

Paul says that godliness with contentment is great gain (v. 6), that if we have food and clothing we should have contentment (v. 8), and that desiring to be rich is to fall into temptation (v. 9).

Our love of money is exposed by the tightness of our grip on what we already have as well as our desire to have more of it. It leads to other kinds of evil. There are people who mistreat their families so they can get more money. There are people who will cheat and steal to accumulate more wealth. There are people who will lie to cover up their insatiable thirst for greater material possessions.

It started with not being content with what they had.

Lest you think I'm only talking about Wall Street bankers, ask yourself these questions:

- How many times each week do you go shopping for something new?
- When you say you "need" to run to the store and get something, what do you mean by "need"?
- How old does your car get before you are convinced it needs to be replaced?
- Are you nervous before your annual review at work because you've been hoping for a raise for months?
- If you went a month with only food and clothing, would you be content? What would you miss most? (I'd miss my house. And my car. And my bed. And barbeque potato chips. And my phone. And Netflix. You know, just to name a few.)
- Has your quest for more in life ever led you to do something you knew was wrong, but you did it anyway?
- What amount of money would you have to make each year to conclude that you made "enough"?

We all struggle with what it means to be content. The reason for this is because we often look at money as a tool to build our own kingdom instead of as a resource to build God's Kingdom.

There's a little phrase in 1 Timothy 6 which if we take it wrong can lead to great selfishness and greed which we justify by quoting this verse.

In 1 Timothy 6:17, Paul states that God "richly provides us with everything to enjoy." Some may read this and conclude that by virtue of possessing, we are now free to utilize our resources in any way we see fit. If we want to be wasteful and self-indulgent in the name of enjoyment, we are justified in so being because God blessed us with wealth for our enjoyment.

In light of the context we've just studied together, I think you can agree there are a few problems with this line of thinking.

First, and obviously, this flies in the face of the entirety of Scripture. With Jesus as the Lord of our lives, He should be calling the shots, not us. Just because we earn a good living does *not* mean we have the right to do whatever we want with our excess because we're wealthy.

Second, we have to at least call into question what we as disciples of Jesus find enjoyable. Some may say if you have the money, give your tithe, and have extra, it's permissible to spend what's left on whatever you'd like for your enjoyment. Many do. We purchase big things for our enjoyment—really nice houses, cars with all the bells and whistles, expensive vacations, boats, four wheelers, and more. But let's not single out those with more resources. Lower income folks can drop a lot of cash on things purely for their enjoyment, too. Smart phones, eating out, movies, and clothing budgets can be justified as needs when in fact they are simply a way of entertaining ourselves.

Personally, I really enjoy eating out. Not having to cook, set the table, clean up, or store left overs is a real treat. I like taking my family out and spending time together over a meal. I really enjoy getting around a table with friends for an evening of eating and laughing. I really enjoy that. I could recite 1 Timothy 6:17 and praise God from my table at Saltgrass Steakhouse six nights a week and justify it all. God gave me my abundance for my enjoyment, I could reason.

While I'm not suggesting a life of ascetic monasticism is the only way to live, I am calling into question what we choose to spend money on based on our enjoyment.

Should we as followers of Christ enjoy anything more than giving? Should we really enjoy stuff more than we enjoy being a blessing to other people? Yes, God gives it to us. Yes, it may be permissible for us to spend money on a new car or a weekend away or a new pair of jeans. But if we use our freedom to spend our resources on things we enjoy, we should at least consider the possibility that we may be enjoying the wrong things.

In other words, what we enjoy says something about the condition of our heart.

———————

There's one more aspect of our attitude toward money that I think warrants our attention—the comparison game. Often, we as wealthy people justify our indulgences because (due to the fact that we earn at a higher rate) we actually give more than someone who earns less. In other words, we've earned the right to be more selfish by making more and giving more. Get what I am saying?

Someone who earns $400,000 annually can spend $300,000 on excessive living and give away $100,000. Compared to a single mom who earns $40,000 but is very disciplined and gives away $10,000, you could argue that the rich person is ten times more generous. It is true that you can do more with $100,000 than $10,000, but that doesn't mean that the person who gives more is more generous.

A problem emerges when we compare our generosity with the generosity of others. Unless you're Warren Buffet, there will always be someone who gave more money away than you. And if you try hard enough, you'll always be able to find someone who gives away less. We're not supposed to compare ourselves with each other.

As Christians, our standard is Christ. He gave everything, and He calls us to surrender everything. He calls us to loosen our grip on what we possess, find contentment what we have, and enjoy the process of digging deeper.

Money is not evil, but the love of it is the root of

all kinds of it. Unfortunately, more of us love it than we're ready to admit. Few of us are truly content. Most of us still cling to what we have, unwilling to loosen our grip.

Meanwhile, God is calling us to sacrifice.

7 | Sacrifice

"And Jesus, looking at him, loved him, and said to him, "You lack one thing: go, sell all that you have and give to the poor, and you will have treasure in heaven; and come, follow me." Mark 10:21

If following Jesus is crazy, I don't want to be sane.

Have you ever met anyone who was just crazy in his or her faith? A Jesus freak? It just didn't make any sense how they lived their lives? All of us know one or two. Maybe it's a co-worker or a friend. When I was in high school, there was the kid named Jeff who walked up and down the hall smiling, shaking hands, and saying, "Praise the Lord." You couldn't help but smile—and think he was a little crazy.

The truth is there aren't that many of those kinds of folks. The reason is as simple as it is alarming.

Many people follow Jesus. Very few *sacrifice* for Jesus. That's not new. It's always been the case. Even when Jesus was on the earth that was true.

Luke 14:25-33 says,

> "Now large crowds were going along with Him; and He turned and said to them, "If anyone comes to Me, and does not hate his own father and mother and wife and children and brothers and sisters, yes, and even his own life, he cannot be My disciple. Whoever does not carry his own cross and come after Me cannot be My disciple. For which one of you, when he wants to build a tower, does not first sit down and calculate the cost to see if he has enough to complete it? Otherwise, when he has laid a foundation and is not able to finish, all who observe it begin to ridicule

him, saying, 'This man began to build and was not able to finish.' Or what king, when he sets out to meet another king in battle, will not first sit down and consider whether he is strong enough with ten thousand men to encounter the one coming against him with twenty thousand? Or else, while the other is still far away, he sends a delegation and asks for terms of peace. So then, none of you can be My disciple who does not give up all his own possessions."

Those are strong words from the Lord Jesus. Crowds followed Jesus everywhere. But every time a crowd assembled, Jesus tried to run some of them off. Read the Gospels. It's true. The danger we face is being a part of the crowd clamoring after Jesus instead of a people sacrificing for Jesus. We all have to answer this question. I hate to ask it because no one wants to face up to it.

What are you giving to God that actually costs you something?

In 2 Samuel 24, we read about an inspiring story involving David and a guy named Araunah the

Jebusite.

King David wants to build an altar on which to make sacrifices. He goes looking for a good spot and finds a promising lead at Araunah's place. We don't know much about Araunah, but it seems like he is a good dude because he offers David the land for free. It's for a good cause, he reasons, and David is *the King* after all. It's the least he could do.

But David's response in 2 Samuel 24:24 is telling. He refuses Araunah's offer flat out.

> "No, but I will surely buy it from you for a price," he said, "for I will not offer burnt offerings to the Lord my God which cost me nothing."

Are we willing to offer up to God a life which costs us nothing? That's comfortable? That's easy? Is that really even an offering?

Romans 12 talks about us giving our lives as sacrifices. No longer do we need an altar on which to offer up animal sacrifices. In the new covenant we worship with our lives. So take the Old Testament principle and lay it on top of the New Testament truth--are you giving anything out of your life that costs you something?

Jesus constantly reminds people who want to follow Him what it will require. Take what He says in Luke 9:23-25 as an example:

> "And He was saying to them all, 'If anyone wishes to come after Me, he must deny himself, and take up his cross daily and follow Me. For whoever wishes to save his life will lose it, but whoever loses his life for My sake, he is the one who will save it. For what is a man profited if he gains the whole world, and loses or forfeits himself?'"

These are words of Jesus, shortly after Peter confesses that Jesus is the Christ. Jesus mentions three things we must do, but really it's all the same thing--sacrifice. Jesus says plainly, "I need you to give something up for me. I need you to offer up to me a sacrifice that *costs* you something."

Often we resist digging deeper into our wallets to meet a need for someone because it's not in our plan or budget. We need to sacrifice. Often we find it difficult to loosen our grip on what is ours because we view our possessions as our own, not as an instrument to build God's Kingdom on earth. We need to sacrifice. Many times we miss out on taking hold of the life that is truly life because we settle for a lesser existence, an existence void of sacrifice.

It's time for us as the church to refuse to live our lives without it costing us something. Luke 9 tells us how to do just that--by denying ourselves, taking up our cross, and following Jesus.

We need to deny ourselves.

This Luke 9 passage is really important. Matthew, Mark, and Luke all include these words of Jesus in their re-telling of His ministry. All three authors put this challenge on the heels of Peter's confession. I believe this is intentional. I believe we are being reminded that many will *say* that Jesus is the Christ, the Son of the Living God. Many people will *claim* that Jesus is their Savior. Few will alter their lives in any substantive way, choosing to live it out in comfort and ease. They don't dare sacrifice.

Jesus uses Peter's confession that He is the Messiah as a teaching point. If you really think He's the Christ, the Lord, the real deal, then you will deny yourself. Just read Mark 8-10. Bookended by the story of two blind guys getting their sight, it's clear the point—even those closest to Jesus didn't get what discipleship really was. It's death, not arguing over the greatest and all that nonsense.

When was the last time you denied yourselves of anything? We are such consumers, we are so wealthy, and we have so much opportunity and luxury at our fingertips. If we want it, we can get it. A bigger something, a faster something, or a shinier something. When was the last time you purposefully did without?

The truth is, few of us ever do.

Do you feel that defensive attitude kicking in? I feel it as I'm writing! I want to explain my selfishness away. I'm not as bad as *some* people. I don't have cable! I drive a rusty, thirteen year old SUV. I haven't eaten out all week! I did stop and get a sweet tea from Sonic last night, though, and bought both my kids a slush. But they're only $1!

You may feel defensive about it, too. I can almost hear you saying it again..."But Titus, I'm not rich." If you live on the poverty line in the U.S., you are among the 10% of the richest people in the world. If you make $50,000, you are in the top 1% of the richest people in the world. We are rich. We have established this fact.

Just as an aside, a lot of people don't think they're rich because of the debt they carry. We sink a lot of cash into stuff we think are necessary that zap us of our ability to be more generous.

I don't know how much money you have in your wallet right now or in your savings account, but it's probably enough to deny yourself of something and instead give to the least of these. It's probably enough that you can afford to dig a little deeper.

If you have eight bucks, for instance, you have a choice. You can subscribe to Hulu Plus for a month or you can buy 25 fruit trees for a poor farmer in Honduras that will yield an annual crop, allowing them to feed their families and sell the rest for income.

If you have $73, you can take your family of four to dinner or you could buy a mobile health clinic for AIDS patients in Uganda. For $2400--and even if you don't have it on hand, that much money enters and leaves your care every month or every year or at some point in your life--you can enjoy four days at an all-inclusive resort or you can fund a generation of education for students in Angola.

I say all this in this way to frame the question differently--when was the last time you deprived yourself of anything? When was the last time you decided to not have so that someone who is hungry or dying or sick could be cared for in a meaningful way?

If you're struggling with all that, consider the words of pastor and author Francis Chan: "God doesn't call us to be comfortable. He calls us to trust Him so completely that we are unafraid to put ourselves in situations where we will be in trouble if He doesn't come through."

To deny ourselves means to be uncomfortable. It means to put ourselves in situations where if God does not come through, we aren't sure what will happen. When was the last time you put yourself in a situation where if God didn't come through, you were going to look crazy?

To deny ourselves is to throw our hands up in the air and admit it: if following Jesus is crazy, we don't want to be sane.

Take up your cross

This is the second thing Luke 9 says we must do if we want to sacrifice for Jesus and His Kingdom. We don't really understand what it means when Jesus says, "Take up your cross" because we have a pretty weird view of the cross these days. We wear it as jewelry, put it in our church buildings as art, and get tattoos of them on our arms. Our 21st century view of the cross is as a reminder of what Jesus did for us. That's a good thing. We need those reminders.

But for the original hearer of Jesus' words (like the ones here in Luke 9), this was not a reminder. It was an invitation. As an instrument of death, the cross was a brutal symbol of suffering, not salvation. It's all well and good that the thought of the cross these days gives us warm fuzzies because of God's great love for us. But next time you see a cross, remember that Jesus calls us to take up one of our own, not just remember His.

Jesus is calling you to get on a cross. We rush to the empty tomb part of the story, but slow down a second. As my mentor and friend Doug Lay says, "The cross is our work. The empty tomb is God's work." In other words, before Jesus can raise us, we have to voluntarily die to ourselves.

In Romans 6, the language Paul uses when he talks about following Jesus is that of death. We die to ourselves so that we can be raised to new life. The problem comes when we think of that death as symbolic, spiritual surrender.

That may be true; it's just not all. What we are saying when we align ourselves with Jesus is that we would be willing to die for Him. That's what everyone in the first century understood. When Jesus said, "Take up your cross" there was no confusion. They were signing up to die.

You may think that sounds crazy. How can you expect someone who is a new Christian to be willing to die for his or her faith? That sounds a little extreme. Is it, though? Eleven of the twelve original disciples died for their faith. It was just part of the deal.

Why isn't it part of our deal? Why do we view ourselves as the exception? One of the most moving experiences of my life was to sit in a room with a couple dozen pastors in India who told story after story after story of persecution, death, and loss. They did not view themselves as exceptional in the slightest. It was just part of following Jesus for them. Not so much for us. Not for me.

Polycarp is my favorite figure in the history of the church. He was the bishop of Smyrna, an understudy of the Apostle John, and an absolute beast of a disciple.

At the age of 86 Polycarp was resting in an upper room of a cottage when the local police arrived at the home. Persecution was common in that day, and Polycarp was a notable leader in the church. They had come to take him away. The historical record says he could've escaped but instead refused to flee, saying, "God's will be done." He went down and spoke with the officials who were quite stunned by his age and devotion. Some of them even wondered why they were sent to seize a man of his noble character.

Polycarp did what any of us would do when confronted with arrest and certain death--he arranged for the men to get something to eat and drink and asked for an hour to pray. He took two hours, but his captors didn't seem to care. Maybe Polycarp had arranged for dessert, and they were distracted.

Finally, they hauled Polycarp to the arena where he would meet the judgment of the Proconsul. The judge attempted to persuade Polycarp to deny his faith. He urged him to swear by Caesar. He begged him to betray Christ, promising to release him if he would do so.

Polycarp's response gives me shivers every time I hear it:

"86 years have I served Him, and He has done me no wrong. How can I blaspheme my King and my Savior?"

Still, the local magistrates tried to convince him. They threatened him with wild animals if he did not repent. Polycarp invited them to turn the beasts loose. They threatened him with fire. Polycarp didn't fear the fire that would burn temporarily, saying, "Bring on whatever you want."

As the crowd gathered wood, Polycarp removed his outer clothes. They started to pin him to a stake with nails and Polycarp responded, "Leave me as I am, for he that gives me strength to endure the fire will enable me not to struggle without the help of your nails." Are you kidding me right now? I would've run as fast as I could in the opposite direction. Polycarp just says, "Well, go ahead and get on with it." Sheesh.

They tied his hands together, Polycarp prayed,

and the fire was lit.

Polycarp's story is hard to fathom. But he was not the first martyr. He wasn't even the first martyr in the town of Smyrna. Thousands of Christians around the world went to the stake before him. Millions have followed since.

People who were following Jesus, who were willing to sacrifice for Jesus, and who were willing to die for Jesus.

It may sound crazy to us, but not because it's never happened before. It sounds crazy because we're not willing to do it. We come up with eighteen reasons not to give fifty cents to a homeless lady, so fathoming our own martyrdom seems insane.

We think of martyrs as exceptional when in fact it should be a given when we sign up to follow Jesus.

In Luke 5, the Apostle Peter left his full nets on the shore to rot in order to follow after Jesus. A couple decades later he was traveling the world preaching the Gospel when he was arrested and sentenced to crucifixion. Peter famously requested to be nailed to a cross upside down.

Peter's faith was intense, unshakable, and resolute.

Why should it be different for us?

Francis Chan tells a story in his book, *Crazy Love,* about wanting to join the Marines. The problem was he didn't want to get up so early, run so far, and work so hard. He wondered about going down to the recruiter's office and proposing a compromise. Maybe he could join up but take it a little easier than the rest of the recruits. He knew that suggesting it would be pointless.

"Everyone knows that if you sign up for the Marines you have to do whatever they tell you. They own you."

Many of us approach faith the same exact way Francis Chan daydreamed about the Marines. Hey, Jesus...I love the forgiveness of sins thing, but would it be okay if I didn't go all-out? I need you to be my Savior, but could we cool it on the "Lord" stuff just a little?

I prefer not to break a sweat, thanks.

If that makes you squirm in your seat, I apologize (not really...I'm not sorry). But why do we think of ourselves as the exception? It's not supposed to be easy. A lot of people come to faith thinking that life is going to get better, easier, and more fun. It's supposed to be *harder*. The worst testimony a Christian can have is that her or his life was hard, they came to Christ, and now everything is a breeze.

That person probably isn't doing something right.

If you are following after Jesus with all you got, that means you have a cross on your back. That's not easy, it's hard. You have to be willing to die.

As pastor Mark Driscoll says, "Jesus doesn't fix everything. He just makes the death more meaningful." Our sacrifice is assumed.

To take up your cross is to say, if following Jesus is crazy, I don't want to be sane.

Follow me

Jesus calls people to follow Him, and it begs this question:

What were they following before?

The people who first heard these words are being asked to give up Judaism. To follow Jesus was to surrender a couple thousand years of religious heritage. Following Jesus was scandalous. He had a different way of doing things.

Most of you reading this aren't Jewish. So what are you following?

Maybe it's the taillights back and forth to the office. You punch the clock, make bank, climb the ladder, and define your life by what you accomplish. Maybe it's a political ideology. You wear the button, cast the votes, attend the rallies, and pray for your candidate to win. If they don't, you're devastated. Maybe it's you. Maybe you wake up in the morning and ask, "What should I do today?" Then you do whatever you feel like. You are your own master.

Here's the truth we must grapple with:

You can't save the world. Politicians can't save the world. Your money and skill and genius cannot save the world. No matter how much of it you have.

Only Jesus can save the world. Why don't we just decide to follow the One who can save the world? Instead of chasing other things, why don't we chase Jesus? Why can't we be as obsessed about Jesus as we are obsessed with so many other things?

I'm coming on strong, I know. Believe me that I've struggled through this stuff myself, so I'm not pointing fingers. And I don't have it all figured it out. In some ways, I'm thinking out loud. But I do know this much:

In following Christ, there aren't many baby steps. Jesus invited people to follow Him, from the start, in complete surrender. Peter leaves his boats without asking a whole lot of questions. Matthew doesn't give his two weeks notice; he just closes up shop and follows Jesus. He gives up what he was following before and follows after Jesus instead.

There are no practice steps.

Some of us need to downsize our lives, reconsider our priorities, sponsor a child living overseas, or maybe even adopt a child and bring them into our home. You might need to go on a mission trip and serve someone in another country, or give your money or time. Give *something*.

When you are following Jesus you have to do something. Something that costs you. Not because it's easy for you, but because it doesn't matter what you think. You're not the boss. You're not in charge. You're following Jesus. He's in charge.

Some of you are thinking that it's impossible. Some of you are thinking you can't do that. Only crazy people can do that. Well Jesus needs some more crazy people. Jesus calls us to be followers who are willing to give anything up, do anything asked, risk anything possible, leverage everything they are to make an impact. People that consider it foolish to cling to that which is lesser.

Jim Elliot famously said, "He is no fool who gives what he cannot keep to gain what he cannot lose." Jim Elliot was slaughtered on a riverbank in Ecuador as he attempted to share the good news about Jesus with people who had never heard it before. He was 29 years old.

If you live like that, people are going to think you are crazy. But if loving Jesus is crazy, I don't want to be sane.

Do you?

8 | Go and Do Likewise

"What good is it, my brothers, if someone says he has faith but does not have works? Can that faith save him?" James 1:14

In Luke 10, Jesus tells the well-known parable about a Good Samaritan. A lawyer stands up and asks Jesus a question. He's not looking to learn anything; he's just trying to trap Jesus. You know the type of guy I mean. Always the smartest guy in the room, he wants to ask a question that really stumps the Prophet.

Trouble is, he's not talking to a mere prophet. The guy asks Jesus what it takes to inherit eternal life. There's that question again. "Hey Jesus, I don't so much care about you, but how can I get myself out of hell?"

Jesus flips the script and asks Mr. Smarty Pants what he thinks. The guy is sharp, and he answers correctly. Love God and love your neighbor as yourself. The lawyer had read Deuteronomy a time or two, it seems. Jesus congratulates him for his answer.

"Do this and you'll live," He replies.

But the poor guy just can't help himself. In fact the Scriptures say he "desires to justify himself." So he asks a follow-up question:

"And who is my neighbor?"

Jesus answers with the story of the Good Samaritan that we all learned when we were kids:

> "...A man was going down from Jerusalem to Jericho, and he fell among robbers, who stripped him and beat him and departed, leaving him half dead. Now by chance a priest was going down that road, and when he saw him he passed by on the other side. So likewise a Levite, when he came to the place and saw him, passed by on the other

side. But a Samaritan, as he journeyed, came to where he was, and when he saw him, he had compassion. He went to him and bound up his wounds, pouring on oil and wine. Then he set him on his own animal and brought him to an inn and took care of him. And the next day he took out two denarii and gave them to the innkeeper, saying, 'Take care of him, and whatever more you spend, I will repay you when I come back.'" (Luke 10:30-35)

When He is done telling the story, Jesus asks the man who in the story proved to be a neighbor to the man who was injured. The good Jewish boy couldn't even bring himself to say "the Samaritan," likely because of his racism against the half-Jewish community. Samaritans were northern Kingdom re-settlers after the Assyrian captivity. They intermarried with their captors and worshipped false Gods. Southern Kingdom Jews hated them for this. That's the short version of the complicated relationship between Jews and Samaritans and likely what causes this guy to not even be able to utter the words, "The Samaritan." So he instead says, "the one who showed him mercy."

Jesus looks at the man and completes his lesson: "You go, and do likewise." A Jew go and do what a Samaritan did? Jesus is being a little cheeky with Mr. Smart Guy here; make no mistake. But he's also very serious. It's a call to action.

There are a lot of important things Jesus says in the story of the Good Samaritan, but none more important than the last: "Go and do likewise."

Anyone with a first grade Sunday school education knows this story. Perhaps that is one of our shortcomings—we know the story all too well. Our familiarity with it causes us to take it for granted. We know what it teaches. We believe that it is true. Too often, our allegiance to these lessons end with our recognition of them.

Jesus did not say, "Go and *think* likewise." He did not suggest we go and *feel* likewise. He certainly did not indicate that what was most important was that we go and *teach* likewise.

We are good at the thinking and the feeling and even the teaching. It's the *doing* that we sometimes struggle with.

Jesus said, "Go and *do* likewise."

I have studied the Scriptures pretty much my whole life. My undergraduate degree is in Bible. My master's degree is in theology. There are a lot of people out there with more Bible knowledge than me, but I think I know more than average. I've spent thousands of hours (and thousands of dollars) accumulating this knowledge.

The only problem is it doesn't matter all that much. Knowing what's right and doing what's right are two different things.

James 1:22 says that we should be "doers of the word, not hearers only." Just three chapters later he underscores this idea again, saying, "Whoever knows the right thing to do and fails to do it, for him it is sin." (James 4:17)

My friends, I've spilled quite a bit of ink in the past several chapters encouraging you to loosen your grip on your stuff and leverage it for a greater good. I have no doubt that if you've read this far you are inclined to agree.

Only selfish jerks don't share. The world is a messed up place. We're all rich whether we think so or not. God wants us to be generous, and there's no good excuse for us to not be. Most of us have at our disposal an incredible tool that we can employ to do much good if only we will let loose. It will take sacrifice, but if we can muster the courage to dig deeper and give up our own comfort we can make an enormous impact.

I have little doubt that you agree with those statements. The only thing left to discuss is not whether or not we believe this, but whether or not we're going to go through the trouble of living it out.

You may be thinking that you've heard all this before. You've read this book, heard this sermon, and watched the tearjerker commercial that begged you for some help. That may very well be true. If so, then the following question should be all the more revealing.

How have you responded?

Nodding your head in agreement as you've read these pages is admirable. But our goal should not be to be admired. Our mission, the work that God has for us, is to love and serve those who live in the margins. This is taking hold of the life that is truly life, as Paul puts it in 1 Timothy 6.

The priest and the Levite were experts in the

Law. They knew their stuff. But that belief did not impact their behavior. Do you want your legacy to be that you believed all the right stuff or do you want your legacy to be that you turned someone's world upside down?

I once served for a week on a short-term missions team to the inner city of Washington, D.C. I led a team of college students, just a handful of us, as we helped an organization in the projects host a daily VBS program for the kids in the neighborhood. Every day a few dozen kids showed up and we told Bible stories and played games and ate snacks.

Present every single day were two boys— DeWayne and DeJean. They were brothers, and I grew pretty attached to them. It's a good thing I liked them, because they hung on me quite often. Perhaps because I was tall or maybe because of my rather misguided head of curly hair, those two kids took a shine to me, too. Piggyback rides were requested and granted several times each day.

Never once did those two boys ask me about

my theology. They weren't curious if I was a Calvinist or Arminian. They did not care if I was a pre-millennial or a post-millennial. They just wanted a piggyback ride and to know someone cared.

At my church we send out several short-term mission teams each year to places all over the world. Once my wife went on a trip with a team to the Dominican Republic, and they went to the community I mentioned earlier called The Hole.

As they made their way down the steep incline and wound there way through the ramshackle buildings, my wife met a little girl named Arianni. She was physically disabled and incapable of moving about like a normal kid.

From the time they arrived in her community until the time they left, my wife and Arianni were bonded together. Every member of that team seemed to have captured a picture of my wife with that little girl in her arms.

Strangely enough, Arianni never asked my wife to sign off on a statement of belief. She did not summon a translator to clear up any theological dissimilarity between them.

She just wanted to be held.

It's been preached and written so often, I could attribute the quote to a half dozen people, "People don't care how much you know until they know how much you care." We need to go and do likewise.

Like I said before, I have two degrees in Bible and theology. I am not saying that what we believe is unimportant. In fact, I am promoting a certain interpretation of Scripture in this book and urging you to believe it. So please don't think I'm minimizing the role of good theology in the life of a Christian.

What I am arguing, and what I believe passages like Luke 10 are arguing, is that we can believe all the right stuff, but if we don't allow our theology to impact our lives then what good is believing it in the first place?

Poet Victor Hugo first said, "You can give without loving, but you cannot love without giving." I agree. What we do matters because it is the manifestation of what we believe. First John 4:20 says,

"If anyone says, 'I love God,' and hates his brother, he is a liar; for he who does not love his brother whom he has seen cannot love God whom he has not seen."

In other words, we can say we love God all we want. But unless we do something about it, we're a bunch of liars.

9 | Surrendering the American Dream

"But our citizenship is in heaven. And we eagerly await a Savior from there, the Lord Jesus Christ."
Philippians 3:20

I was tired of being a liar. So was my wife. We had been reading the Bible and some other really convicting books, listening to sermons and mulling some things over. We were tired of saying we loved God a lot but not doing too much to show it.

Then I sat down in a planning meeting with our staff at church, and we began to talk about an all-church emphasis we were going to tackle in the fall. Our lead guy started laying out the big idea and as we talked and prayed and planned, I started to feel a deep sense of conviction that God was going to call me to do something risky. He was going to call me to sacrifice.

He was going to call me to let loose, dig deep, and take hold of the life that is really life.

As we planned for months the series that became known as *All In*, my wife and I continued to talk about what was next for us. What was God calling us to do? We weren't sure. Then the fall came and our church experienced *All In* together. In fact, chapter seven of this book is loosely based on a sermon I gave during that series. We still weren't totally sure what we were doing, but we had just determined that we were supposed to do *something*.

So we did, and I'd like to tell you about it, lest you think I am preaching a bunch of stuff that I'm not practicing.

Let me back up a little bit first.

Most people in ministry complain a lot about not making very much money. I've never been one of them because I know it's not true. I make more than the average youth minister in America, based on one survey I saw at least. And it was on the

Internet, so it has to be true. Plus, I remember when my dad shoveled horse manure for a living and sometimes we started our car *and* changed the channel on our television with a pair of vice grips. So you won't catch me complaining (About how much I make, that is. I'll still probably complain about other things).

A few years ago my family and I moved to Texas. I had heard the saying, "Everything's bigger in Texas" and sure enough, it is. We had some very generous folks help us put a down payment in on a house. So we settled into our little McMansion without giving it a whole lot of thought. It was the nicest house I had ever lived in by far. Only a few years old, the house my wife and I purchased had four bedrooms, two and a half baths, two living spaces, two areas to eat in, two living rooms, and a two-car garage. It was typical of a Texas house, but still pretty sweet digs.

I was 30. My wife was 28. We had two kids. Our fence wasn't white and picket, but other than that it was a big old slice of Americana. We were living the life. Then a crazy thing happened on our way to the American dream.

In short, the *All In* series happened, and sped up

some decision-making we'd been stalling out on. We realized we were filthy stinking rich. Not by Katy, Texas standards. I already mentioned how the average household in the county our church is located in makes over $100,000 each year. We do not. But by the world's standards, we are wealthy. No question.

We reviewed the stats in a previous chapter.

There are over 2 billion people in the world who live on two bucks a day or less. My salary put me *easily* in the 1% of the richest people on the planet and in the top 7 million richest people overall. That's a youth minister's money, folks.

Basically we stacked up all the info that you've read in this book and considered it prayerfully. What were we going to personally do about our brothers and sisters living all around the world? We already gave away money to our church. We sponsored a kid through Compassion International. I kept change in my ashtray to give to homeless folks, even the liars. By all accounts we were fairly generous folks. Still, we felt like we were being called to do something else.

We felt as though we were not giving enough money away. We needed to loosen our grip. We were living in a 2,600-plus square foot expenditure that prevented us from being as generous as we wanted to be. So the first thing we decided to do is sell our house and downsize to a rental. The monthly savings would net us well over $500 a month, which we planned to give away. We sat down and figured out how much more we were going to give to our church and then picked a few other things we wanted to make commitments to.

Some of you are thinking, "Oh, sweet. I did that a couple years back. It's a no-brainer. What took you so long, dummy?" I'm thankful for folks like you. In fact, it's seeing the generosity of others that really pushed us over the edge. We weren't the first people in the history of the universe to purposefully downsize. It was inspirational.

Others thought we were a little nuts, for economic or other reasons. Who rents these days? Why throw your money away? You're house isn't *that* big! If you can afford it, what's the harm? Why move? Won't your smaller house feel crowded? That kind of stuff.

We thought about it from every possible angle. And I'd be a liar if I told you we were totally cool with every aspect of the decision. But we had reached some conclusions that superseded all our reservations, conclusions that won't shock you if you've read this far:

- We were paying big money for rooms we barely used while there are homeless people all over the world (Luke 14:13-14, Proverbs 19:17).
- We had two eating areas in our home. Tens of thousands of people died of starvation or starvation-related causes yesterday and it will happen again today. That was not okay with us (Matthew 25:35, Proverbs 28:27).
- Investments in this world matter way less than investments in the Kingdom of God, so owning a home just wasn't a huge priority for us anymore (Proverbs 14:31, Proverbs 11:24).
- By downsizing our space, we were reminding ourselves that this world isn't really our home (Philippians 3:20, Hebrews 13:14).
- Capitalism is a great financial system, but it's not a basic tenet of Christianity. It may be the means through which two formerly

poor kids like us gathered up a lot of stuff, but that doesn't mean we deserve it or have the right to hoard it (Matthew 6:19-21, Matthew 25:40).

So our lives were reduced by about 1,200 square feet. Our extra dining space, our extra bathroom, and our extra living room all disappeared. The key word there is "extra." Since our house got smaller, so did our collection of things. We must've donated 100 bags and boxes of stuff we didn't have room for any more. We sold half our furniture – our excess dining room table, excess furniture, a big entertainment center, and more.

We increased our monthly giving to our church by about a third, started sponsoring another kid through *G.O. Ministries,* and began investing in a few other ministries we believed in. I don't say that for a pat on the back. I just wanted to tell you I really do believe this stuff I'm writing about.

We also decided to take some of the capital we'd gained in selling our home and start a nonprofit organization. I'll tell you about that in a minute. Best of all, we created margin in our lives so that when we are approached with a need we don't have to say "no" any more. Instead, we almost always say "yes."

We landed in a home that, globally, is still above average. The point was never to live in squalor. The goal was to leverage our wealth for the good of the Kingdom, not to inundate ourselves with meaningless trinkets and possessions.

The decision to sell our house and give more money away was our conviction. It may not be everyone's. In fact, when we went through *All In* people in our church responded in a lot of different ways. Some folks committed to giving more money the poor, others decided to adopt orphans, and others made commitments related to spiritual disciplines. When we're open to God's leading in our lives, there are lots of valid responses. One of ours was to sell our home, but that certainly doesn't make us better than anyone else. There are many people who will give more money away than us next year because they earn more or spend less or both. Again, I'm not interested in the comparison game. I think we can agree on this point: While our convictions about *what* to do may vary, there is a challenge for every single person who calls himself or herself a Christ follower.

- Are you more loyal to Jesus than you are to your wealth?
- Have you pledged allegiance to Christ's Kingdom above and beyond any other kingdom, including your own personal realm?
- Have you accepted the Gospel simply as a means to achieve your personal salvation or have you accepted it as your marching orders, prompting in you a different way of living?

Pastor and author David Platt challenges us this way:

"Anyone wanting to proclaim the glory of Christ to the ends of the earth must consider not only how to declare the Gospel verbally but also how to demonstrate the Gospel visibly in a world where so many are urgently hungry."

If the Gospel is just a means to attain personal salvation, no action is required. No life change is demanded. No sacrifice is called for. But if the Gospel serves as our marching orders as Christ followers, then we all need to determine what Jesus is calling us to do.

And it may not be easy.

I don't want to swoop in, stir the pot with the Scriptures and quotes and mild rants, and then swoop out, leaving confusion and guilt in my wake. That's not my goal at all. If you are considering giving up on the whole American dream thing, I'd like to give you a few things to think about as you consider how God is calling you to change your life.

1. Sit down and read some Scripture. Luke 14:13-14, Proverbs 19:17, Matthew 25:35, Philippians 3:20, Hebrews 13:14, and other quoted passages scattered throughout this book were instrumental in transforming our thinking.

2. Look yourself up on the Global Rich List website. Just Google it. Punch in your salary and see where you rank. Scroll down and get some analysis on how the rest of the world lives by comparison.

3. Have a nice honest talk with yourself, with

God, and with your family. Do you have enough? Too much? Who gets to say so?

4. Do some soul-searching on how you justify those areas of excess. Why do you think you need the things you think you need? Is it normal in your community? Can you afford it? Have you ever really even stopped to think about it?

5. After you are done doing all that, determine to do something that other people won't understand in order to advance the Kingdom. How can you leverage your wealth to be more generous and beneficial to Kingdom work?

I know we've covered this verse before, but let me run it past you one more time:

> "Command those who are rich in this present world not to be arrogant nor to put their hope in wealth, which is so uncertain, but to put their hope in God, who richly provides us with everything for our enjoyment. Command them to do good, to be rich in good deeds, and ***to be generous***

and willing to share. (Emphasis is mine) In this way they will lay up treasure for themselves as a firm foundation for the coming age, so that they may take hold of the life that is truly life." (1 Timothy 6:17-19)

My family is done ignoring those words. We're done pretending we're not rich. We're done hoarding our wealth. We're done living for the present age. We're going to live with less because less will do, and give more because we have plenty to spare.

I was not given a lot so I could sit back and enjoy my loot. Neither were you. To the victor goes the spoil is a great quote, until you realize that all the spoils eventually spoil. Then the somewhat less inspiring quote applies: "to the victor goes a bunch of rotten, rusty stuff."

Jesus himself said it best,

"Do not lay up for yourselves treasures on earth, where moth and rust destroy and where thieves break in and steal, but lay up for yourselves treasures in heaven, where neither moth nor rust destroys and where thieves do not break in and steal" (Matthew 6:19-20).

Maybe stewardship that honors Christ is not about living within our means, but leveraging our means to help others live. Maybe when we loosen our grip on our American dream we can take hold of that which really matters. Maybe we are called to surrender what's less important so that we can gain what matters most.

10 | Don't Be a Goat

"'He judged the cause of the poor and needy; then it was well. Is not this to know me?' declares the Lord.'" Jeremiah 22:16

Have you ever been around goats?

I grew up on farms. We lived on a couple hundred acres, then we moved to a place with only a couple dozen. When my family finally bought a place of our own we still had three acres and so always had a few animals around. I was a teenager by then.

When I was young I viewed the animals as

pets. We had a dog named Tasha and later a dog named Scamp. I had a pig that I'm sure was probably named Wilbur because, well, obviously. My sister had a pig named Sandy. I'll never forget the day I came home from school and Wilbur was gone but Sandy was still there.

I mourned him.

A few weeks later I ate him.

I love bacon (To be precise, I love bacon, beef, and beef wrapped in bacon).

Farming was a means of survival. We ate the eggs we got from our chickens and the beef we got from our cattle. We baled hay that fed our animals. We stopped short of knitting our own sweaters from our sheep's wool. It was the 1980s, after all, not the 1880s.

We did have some sheep, though. My sister and I were in 4-H and FFA, and we both raised sheep to show at the county fair. I'm not trying to brag, but I got Grand Champion one year. More on that in a second.

We also had a goat once.

In recent years goats have gotten together and hired a decent PR firm to remake their image. Goat's milk is all the rage with people who wear flannel and live off the grid. The same people likely churn their own butter. I imagine that all of them live in the rural parts of western Canada and blog about being better than everyone else. In this way, goats have a hipster appeal that almost makes them seem kind of cool.

I assure you, goats are not cool.

When we had that thing I spent about half of my time trying to keep from getting chewed on by a goat and the other half of my time being chewed on by a goat. We kept the goat in a pen next to our garage, and I think the devilish creature ate its way through the wall and then consumed our family automobile.

Goats are not cool; they are four-legged agitators with plans take over the world. Be on your guard. Nothing can stop them. It's infuriating.

We finally got rid of the goat because that's the best thing you can do with a goat – get rid of it. The highlight of owning a goat is that you can then sell the goat. If you drink goat's milk, more power to you. I'm sure it's delicious. I will stick with cow milk. They don't try to nibble on my shoes and hair.

Sheep are much better.

My sister is a year older and was the first to get a sheep. She named him Lanny, though his legal name was Lanny the Lamb. I think Lanny was short for lanolin, the waxy substance secreted by the sebaceous glands of wool-bearing animals. If you didn't know that, you're likely a city kid. You probably don't like going on hayrides, either, because "it's itchy."

I'm not judging.

Lanny was great. He sort of acted like a human because we didn't have any other sheep around; it was just him. My sister would walk him around like a dog on a leash, and when the weather was nice we'd hook his leash onto our clothesline, and he would move around and play with us in the yard.

For you city kids who kept reading even though I already offended you, a clothesline is a cord or string you would stretch between two trees or a clothesline pole to hang your wet clothes on to dry. They are enjoying a resurgence because they're considered "green." Especially up in western Canada with the butter churners. Anyway, we had one and we would hook Lanny to it.

Sheep aren't the smartest creatures in the world, but they aren't demon possessed like goats. In the decade of my childhood where I was pretty consistently around sheep I only wanted to kill a couple of them. There was one that bleated like a seventy-five year old woman who had chain smoked for decades (think Joan Rivers with four legs and chewing her own cud). At times humorous, I did want to harm her on a couple of occasions.

By contrast, I think all goats should die a swift, merciless death. No apologies. Let them munch on the inside of their own caskets for all eternity.

I got my first lamb the following year. I don't remember what I named him, and I don't remember him being as cool as Lanny was, but I enjoyed raising him and showing him at the county fair that August. I tell you all this to say one thing, really:

If you have to choose, be a sheep.

Whatever you do, don't be a goat.

————————

There is no passage in the Scripture that has influenced me more in the past few years than

Matthew 25:31-46. I wanted to take a minute and break it down for you, too, as you think about your next steps in letting loose of your wealth so you can take hold of the life that really is life.

> "When the Son of Man comes in his glory, and all the angels with him, then He will sit on his glorious throne. Before Him will be gathered all the nations, and He will separate people one from another as a shepherd separates the sheep from the goats. And He will place the sheep on His right, but the goats on the left." (Matthew 25:31-33)

Here we see a picture of the coming of Christ. I'll let theologians debate the where and when. I'm concerned here with what happens upon His glorious return. What appears to be of chief concern is separating the nations into two groups. He identifies the categories as sheep and goats. Sheep to the right, goats to the left, Jesus has something to say to each.

> "Then the King will say to those on His

right, 'Come, you who are blessed by my Father, inherit the kingdom prepared for you from the foundation of the world. For I was hungry and you gave me food, I was thirsty and you gave me drink, I was a stranger and you welcomed me, I was naked and you clothed me, I was sick and you visited me, I was in prison and you came to me.' Then the righteous will answer him, saying, 'Lord, when did we see you hungry and feed you, or thirsty and give you drink? And when did we see you a stranger and welcome you, or naked and clothe you? And when did we see you sick or in prison and visit you?' And the King will answer them, 'Truly, I say to you, as you did it to one of the least of these my brothers, you did it to me.'" (Matthew 25:34-40)

To the sheep the King says "Thank you." They fed him, gave Him a drink, clothed Him when He was naked, and welcomed Him when He was a stranger. They visited Him when He was sick and in prison. Their blessing awaits.

The sheep people take exception to this, or at least are a little confused by it. Seems like they would remember giving the God of the Universe a sandwich. They ask what in the world he's talking about. His response is simple. When they did it for "the least of these my brothers" they did it to him.

Then Jesus turns His attention to those gnarly goats on His left.

> "Depart from me, you cursed, into the eternal fire prepared for the devil and his angels. For I was hungry and you gave me no food, I was thirsty and you gave me no drink, I was a stranger and you did not welcome me, naked and you did not clothe me, sick and in prison and you did not visit me.' Then they also will answer, saying, 'Lord, when did we see you hungry or thirsty or a stranger or naked or sick or in prison, and did not minister to you?'
> Then He will answer them, saying, 'Truly, I say to you, as you did not do it to one of the least of these, you did not do it to me.' And these will go away into eternal punishment, but the righteous into eternal life."

This harsh speech has the same outline as the one the sheep got, but with a negative tone. Rather than blessing, the goats are cursed. They refused to do for Jesus what the sheep had done. They gave Him no food, no drink, no clothing. They did not visit Him or welcome Him.

They object, arguing they'd never had the opportunity. It was unfair to punish them for a lack of action when the action required was never a possibility. How were they supposed to serve Him in this way? Jesus' response is terse and jarring:

"When you were not doing those things for the least of these, you were not doing it for me. Now go to hell."

I am telling you, you don't want to be a goat. Be a sheep instead. Matthew 25 should serve as every Christian's inspiration for generous living. It is not guilt or compulsion that motivates us. Rather, serving and obeying Jesus is motivation enough. There are six categories of people He calls the "least of these" and urges us to help:

- The hungry
- The thirsty
- The sick
- The naked
- The stranger
- The imprisoned

Do you need to be further convinced that we have a mandate to help these six groups of people? If nothing I've said prior to now was motivation enough, does it change anything to recognize that when I say we should serve the poor what I'm really saying is that we should serve Jesus? Just in case you're not quite ready to let loose, dig deep, or take hold, let's take one last look at the needs that exist in these areas.

———————

The Hungry

Over 800 million people in the world don't have enough food to eat. The vast majority of this population lives in developing countries. Poor nutrition causes nearly half of all deaths among children under five annually.

Frustratingly, the world produces enough food to properly care for the entire population (lots of studies support this, including one from the University of Minnesota that claims we produce enough food to support a population of over ten million.) It's estimated that $3.2 billion is needed per year to reach all the hungry school-age children in the world. If the entire population of America pitched in $10 per year that amount would be exceeded easily. We don't have a production problem; we have a sharing problem. We have a problem loosening our grip.

Jesus says feed the hungry. Don't be a goat.

The Thirsty

Not surprisingly, over 800 million people also lack access to clean, safe drinking water. Twice as many people as that don't have basic sanitation at their disposal. It is estimated that the women in underdeveloped nations spend more than 40 billion hours annually retrieving and carrying water.

Every twenty seconds, a child dies from a water-related illness. Drilling a well costs about $3,000 and can serve a community for generations. We don't need to come up with an idea to solve this problem; we just need to solve the problem.

Jesus says provide water for the thirsty. Don't be a goat.

The Naked

Rather famously, TOMS shoes gives away a pair of shoes for every pair it sells. To date, they have given away more than 10 million pairs of shoes. It is hard to believe that we live in a world where people are so poor they may not have clothes to wear. If you've visited a third world country, however, you know that it's the truth. Meanwhile, my closet and drawers burst forth with shirts I hardly wear.

Jesus says provide clothing for the naked. Don't be a goat.

The Sick

216 million children have died before they turned five years old since 1990. Tragically, most of these deaths are due to preventable diseases. Sicknesses like pneumonia and diarrhea are the biggest killers, claiming the lives of almost 5,000 kids every single day. In the developed world these afflictions barely slow us down because we have multiple ways of treating them. However, in many places they are a death sentence.

Jesus says we should help the sick. Don't be a goat.

The Stranger

As I write this in 2014, about nine million Syrians have fled their homes since unrest broke out in their country three years ago. This is a staggering number. Worldwide in 2013, over 15 million people worldwide were the recipients of services as registered refugees. Immigration reform is an important and controversial topic in America, and unfortunately political convictions influence our thinking more often than the Scripture. I know this to be true because I live in Texas. I would challenge all believers to look at how the Scriptures teach us to treat foreigners and strangers. Lots of challenging stuff.

Jesus says welcome the stranger. Don't be a goat.

The Imprisoned

In context, this admonishment is likely referring to those being held against their will because of their faith. In this regard, we know that about 200 million Christians around the world suffer from some form of persecution. We have an obligation not to turn a deaf ear to those brothers and sisters.

If Jesus truly came to free the captives, we must also think of those being bought and sold like property. Slavery is not abolished in our world. More than 20 million people are in chains. And while we're caring about people who are imprisoned, we may as well include the over 2 million people who are incarcerated in the United States. It may be hard to muster sympathy for criminals, but if we believe the Gospel we won't neglect to minister to those in prison.

Don't be a goat.

I already told you about why we sold our house,
wanting to give away more money and all that.
Another calling we felt was to take some of our
profits and start a nonprofit organization. So I filled
out some paperwork and submitted it to the IRS
and the State of Texas and our new nonprofit
organization was born. I felt like we were being
called to go *All In*, not *Some In,* so why not?

We call it The 25 Group. The "25" is a tip of the
cap to Matthew 25, and our organization is
extremely concerned with obeying the command of
Jesus in Matthew 25 to care for the least of these.
Our purpose is to leverage wealth to do good,
encouraging individuals and companies to loosen
their grip on their excess to help other people who
are hungry and thirsty and sick. The challenge to
individuals is to give $25 each month. If hundreds
of people do this, we're able then to make
significant capital investments in ministries who
are on the front lines doing all of the above—
feeding the sick, providing clean drinking water to

the thirsty, and more.

A rush of adrenaline surged through my body when I opened an e-mail after our giving community had been operating for only about three months. We had already sent several thousand dollars to a ministry partner in India, and the e-mail contained pictures of kids dancing around the clean flow of water spilling out of their village's new well.

The next week I visited a nutrition center in the Dominican Republic (not far from The Hole) where about 70 kids are fed a decent meal once a day, six days a week. Funds collected by The 25 Group were going to meet this need, and it was a thrill to see it first hand.

As we grow, we are looking to meet the needs of the least of these in the United States and around the world. I'm a full-time pastor, so we're using our spare time to keep up the website and make phone calls and try to raise money that can be leveraged to help people who are starving and lonely and being held captive.

We're just getting started. Our goal is to give away $100,000 this year and $1 million dollars by the end of our third year. We want to drill more wells and fund more nutrition centers and make significant donations to organizations battling human trafficking and investing in the lives of the least of these.

We're not throwing money at a problem, we're linking arms with people who personally know the names of the kids they serve. We're investing in sustainable solutions which will continue to serve people decades from now. In the village where we funded the water well we are also funding the construction of a school building. Our long-term goal is to partner closely with this village, seeing to it that they don't do without.

Two years ago I was sitting in my 2700 square foot house chomping on potato chips, watching my big screen television and not thinking twice about the fact that I was holding on to my comfort, wealth, and way of life too tightly. I had no idea I needed to let loose, dig deep, and take hold of that which was really life.

These days a day never passes without me thinking about those around the world who are hungry and thirsty and naked and sick and a stranger and in prison. I'm leveraging relationships, finances, and spare time to try to make an impact.

Not because I'm better than anyone else.

Not because I have it all figured out.

I just don't want to be a goat.

| Conclusion

Now that all the stats and stories have been
spilled forth, it's my job to leave you with a
challenge and some encouragement. I always feel
more motivated after receiving a little pep talk, so
before I give you some practical ideas on what to do
next, let me encourage you.

First of all, we all need to realize that it's
working. Generosity is making an enormous
difference in this world. God's people and other
like-minded folks are making an impact. Sixty years
ago, almost every nation in the world was poor.
Philanthropist Bill Gates recently suggested that
there would be very *few* poor nations by 2035. A
big reason for this is the work of faith-based

organizations all around the world. I want to acknowledge here that eliminating poverty is not the primary mission of the church. However, it is an act of justice we are commanded to participate in as a response to the Gospel. Just because it's not our *primary* mission doesn't mean it's not an *important* mission. Jesus's primary mission was to seek and save that which was lost, but He did not go around ignoring people's needs.

When I was just starting out as a youth minister fifteen years ago, we did a thing called 30 Hour Famine. A big selling point of that event was how over 30,000 kids died every day because of starvation or starvation-related causes. To purposefully go without food was a challenge, but miniscule in light of what was going on around the world. Now, a decade and a half later, 30 Hour Famine reports that less than 20,000 kids die each day. That's still way too many, but the stat has been cut nearly in half. That's progress, in large part because of foreign aid and sponsorship programs that provide basic needs for kids and their families. The church led the way.

Some don't want to give to certain causes because they're afraid it's an unwise investment.

Like a cynical citizen who doesn't want to vote because they don't think it will make a difference, we cling tightly to our money because we don't think that charity makes a difference.

If you think this way, send me an email. I'll send back pictures of children in India getting a sparkling clean drink of water out of the well that ninety complete strangers donated to them through The 25 Group.

If you think it doesn't matter, come to my church some Saturday morning. You don't have to do anything, just sit and watch while volunteers hand out over 100 boxes of food to the needy in our community. I think what you'll hear is a lot of gratitude. You might even see a tear or two shed.

My preacher growing up was a guy named Rod Farthing. He now serves in a prison ministry known as American Rehabilitation Ministries, or A.R.M. No one cares much about prisoners in our country. It's an awful system, even if it is a necessary one, with corruption and pain and very few success stories. A.R.M. does a lot, but one of the biggest things they do is send Bible studies into prisons for inmates to use. Rod told me recently of two individuals who had been transformed by their outreach. One man was moved to reach out to the Zapateo people of southern Mexico upon his release. Another in a federal prison became a passionate follower of Christ and baptized over 200 fellow inmates. One of them went on to be a prison chaplain upon his release and has led many other people to Christ.

If you don't think that loosening our grip on our wealth and giving more freely makes an impact in the lives of people all around this world, then how do you explain the transformation we see in so many ways?

There are orphans being welcomed into families, children being fed a nutritious meal, and a new person being provided clean drinking water every 30 seconds. Girls who have been trafficked for sex are being rescued and loved and taught a skill so they don't feel like they have to return to a life of slavery just to survive. Desperately sick people are being made well through generous donations. I know of one ministry in India that served over 72,000 people in their mission hospital in a single year. American doctors donated their time to perform 105 cleft lip and palate surgeries for children in India in just a few days.

If you don't think us letting loose, digging deep, and taking hold of what really matters is making a difference, you are mistaken.

Sadly mistaken.

It *does* make a difference. And it seems like the whole world is starting to figure this out.

The Giving Pledge is a loose association of over 100 billionaires who have committed to give away at least half their dynastic wealth in their lifetime or in their will. Rich people have always been generous, but this is different. They all simply agree that their excess is more useful to someone else than themselves. They have the mansions and the cars and the vacations and the toys. And then some. They are committed to giving the "then some" to people who need it more than they do.

Sure, they are richer than most. But if the church should be the most generous group of people on earth, then why aren't we giving away our "then some?" Even if it's less of a "then some," we need to loosen our grip on it.

It is easier than ever to give. Google "charity" and you'll fetch over 96 million results. Anybody with a credit card or a cell phone can give online, by text, or even by purchasing other products that are tied to a cause.

If you're a part of a church, you've already got a conduit for your funds. Chances are, your church is doing a lot of great stuff in your community and around the world. If not, maybe God is calling you to be a trailblazer. Give generously to the local church and the efforts in your own community. It's that simple.

I think the main reason generosity is on the rise is because we're sick and tired of being selfish, materialistic people. We are arguably the most prosperous people in history. We've even invented words to describe our cozy yet conflicted socio-economic status, words like "affluenza" and "stuffocation." There is pretty good evidence that the more wealthy a society is the more unhappy it becomes. There's never been a grumpier, more crotchety, collectively disagreeable America than there is today.

And we've never had more than we do.

The solution being offered by so many (including me) is to turn from our idols of self and stuff and turn instead to sacrifice and generosity. Take hold of the life that is truly life—not a life meant to gratify every materialistic whim, but one devoted to doing for the least of these what Jesus says we should do. Anyone who's had the experience of walking down a dusty street in a third world country, granting a piggy back ride to an inner-city youth, or hugging a teary-eyed single mother struggling to make ends meet knows that life is about way more than building our own little kingdoms.

We were kidding ourselves for decades, building the American dream on the basis of bulging wallets and indulgent lifestyles. But we're wising up as a nation and, I think, as a church. The epidemic of materialism has found it's antidote, and it's being injected into human hearts all over this great country. The legacy we leave in our wake will be one of kindness, purpose, and transformation.

There may just be hope for us yet.

First, we must let loose, dig deep, and take hold of the life that is truly life.

| Disclaimers & Shout-Outs

What you just read was a trip out on a limb in a lot of ways.

For one thing, everything was written in one week. Five days, really. From Monday, May 12 to Friday, May 16, 2014, I spent most of my waking hours pouring over these pages. That may sound a little nutty (and it may explain the less coherent thoughts you came across), but the reason for it is actually pretty simple. As a husband, dad, pastor, Executive Director, and semi-regular blogger, it is next to impossible to find any time to work on longer form writing. I had a week of vacation already approved. My wife was going to be out of town visiting some friends. I would have all day while my kids were at school plus early mornings and late nights to work. I could've watched Netflix all week, but I decided to try and write a book instead.

As you can imagine, writing even a short book in a few days is a challenge. I have to confess to having employed some cheat codes. These writing hacks, if you will, involve recycling some old blog and sermon content from the past couple of years. Unless you are a loyal reader of my blog who also happens to attend my church you won't notice, but I just would have felt kind of sleazy not admitting to it. The truth is, this entire book is about three years of thinking that has finally made its way onto paper, so it kind of made sense to employ some old thoughts. It's been a journey. Still is.

A final challenge is that there is no way to deal with a complex subject like generosity in a comprehensive, authoritative manner. There is a ton of Scripture in the pages you just read, but what you are holding in your hands is not the final word on anything. I am confident that while you are reading you're going to think of an angle I don't address.

In some ways, this is the exact response I

desire from readers. If I provoke more questions than I answer, I will view that as a victory. Whether or not you agree with everything I say is immaterial to me. I just hope you find the content engaging and that it sparks some conversations among your family and friends. Additionally, this is a self-published work. I hope you can look past my formatting flubs and literary failures and hear my heart on this complicated topic.

In short, what this little experiment was meant to produce was a thought-provoking, honest, humble conversation starter. If I've challenged an assumption, raised some important questions, or got you thinking about doing something crazy, then I've accomplished my goal.

Too many people have informed my personal journey on this topic to name them all. They are family and friends and preachers and teachers. Thanks to each for the theological conversations, hearty debate, and occasional heated disagreement on this subject. In my office there are five picture frames. They each hold an image of a man who has made me who I am. Thanks dad, Rod, Prof Lay, Shan, and my three best buddies Keith, Lucas, and Matt. I have had the privilege of calling many men preacher, professor, mentor, and friend, but if they all played a concert you guys would be the headliners.

Huge shout out to the English Standard Version of the Holy Bible, from which I quoted a few times. If I didn't quote from the ESV it was the NIV. This being a self-published work and all, I'm not confident I did that citation right just then, but I'm pretty sure I'm supposed to say which version I used in the book – so there you go.

To my beautiful wife Kari—my greatest calling in life is being your husband and I'm so proud to live out that calling. You are my best thing and I love chasing after Jesus with you. Thanks for believing in me and never making me feel bad for loving Christ's church.

To Nora and Malachi, being your daddy is such a thrill. I pray I can live well and point you toward Jesus, and I pray you read this book more than once and live it out for the rest of your lives. You are such intelligent, softhearted, joy-filled kids. Thanks for all the laughs, wrestling matches, fashion shows, and trampoline sessions.

To the many nameless faces who have instructed me experientially, from the dumps of Delhi to the streets of Santiago to the markets of Mexico City and the inner city of St. Louis, Houston, Washington D.C., and more, thank you. Meeting you and knowing you has been a great honor. You may at times feel ignored, oppressed, or without hope in this world. If I do nothing else in my life, it will be to ensure that you do not feel that way forevermore.

| About the Author

Titus Benton is a pastor all the time and a writer and Executive Director the rest of the time. He blogs regularly at www.tituslive.com and would love to connect on Twitter (@TitusLive).

The author's entire share of the profits of this book are being donated to The 25 Group. To find out more about the work of this nonprofit community, you can visit www.the25group.org and keep in touch via Facebook (www.facebook.com/the25group) or Twitter (@the25group).

Made in the USA
Charleston, SC
04 October 2014